Domestic Environmental Labour

This book addresses the question of domestic environmental labour from an ecofeminist perspective. A work of cultural geography, it explores the proposition that the practice and politics of domestic labour being undertaken in the name of 'the environment' needs to be better recognized, understood and accounted for as a phenomenon shaped by, and shaping of, gender, class and spatial relations.

The book argues that a significant yet neglected phenomenon worthy of research attention is the upsurge in voluntary, and yet mostly unrecognized, domestic environmental labour in high-consuming households in late modernity, with the burden often falling on women seeking to green their lives and homes in aid of a sustainable planet. Further, because domestic environmental labour is undervalued in governance and the formal economy, much like other types of domestic labour, householders have become an unrecognized and unaccounted-for supply of labour for the greening of capitalism.

Situated within broad global debates on links between ecological and social change, the book has relevance in the many jurisdictions around the world in which households are positioned as sites of environmental protection through green consumption. The volume engages existing interest in household environmental behaviour and practice, advancing understanding of these topics in new ways.

Carol Farbotko is a researcher in cultural geography, with interests in conceptualizing and analyzing the ways in which culture shapes, and is shaped by, environmental change. She has studied the cultural politics of a range of human and non-human subjects.

T0347544

Routledge Explorations in Environmental Studies

For a full list of titles, please visit:
www.routledge.com/Routledge-Explorations-in-Environmental-Studies/book-series/REES

Rawls and the Environmental Crisis
Dominic Welburn

A Green History of the Welfare State
Tony Fitzpatrick

The Governance of Green Urban Spaces in the EU
Social Innovation and Civil Society
Judith Schicklinski

NGO Discourses in the Debate on Genetically Modified Crops
Ksenia Gerasimova

Sustainability in the Gulf
Challenges and Opportunities
Edited by Elie Azar and Mohamed Abdelraouf

Environmental Human Rights
A Political Theory Perspective
Edited by Markku Oksanen, Ashley Dodsworth and Selina O'Doherty

African Philosophy and Environmental Conservation
Jonathan O. Chimakonam

Domestic Environmental Labour
An Ecofeminist Perspective on Making Homes Greener
Carol Farbotko

Domestic Environmental Labour

An Ecofeminist Perspective on Making Homes Greener

Carol Farbotko

LONDON AND NEW YORK

First published 2018
by Routledge

2 Park Square, Milton Park, Abingdon, Oxfordshire OX14 4RN
52 Vanderbilt Avenue, New York, NY 10017

Routledge is an imprint of the Taylor & Francis Group, an informa business

First issued in paperback 2019

British Library Cataloguing-in-Publication Data
A catalogue record for this book is available from the British Library

Library of Congress Cataloging-in-Publication Data
A catalog record for this book has been requested

ISBN: 978-1-138-77774-3 (hbk)
ISBN: 978-0-367-87001-0 (pbk)

Typeset in Times New Roman
by Deanta Global Publishing Services, Chennai, India

For Reuben, Leo, Meriseta, Wally and TK.

Contents

1 Introduction

The mysterious absence of domestic environmental labour

Domestic labour is as ancient as humankind itself. Domestic labour is observable across space and time. It takes on myriad forms across different cultural and geographic milieu, and is associated with a vast range of different technologies. It involves complex socio-ecological systems within and beyond the domestic. Domestic labour is the work involved in carrying out, either personally or by enrolling others, those everyday activities that sustain life. Accessing and using water to wash and bathe. Finding, nurturing, distributing and processing plants and animals to eat, and materials to clothe, house, transport and entertain members of a household or commune, particularly young ones. Keeping dirt from bodies, dwellings, clothing and other possessions at bay. Sourcing energy for cooking, heating and cooling.

What counts as domestic, at least for my purposes as a cultural geographer, is both fluid and broad. Having already referred to 'household' and 'commune' and 'dwelling', it is important to point out that domestic labour can be conducted in any place where people organize access to water, shelter, food and so on in their usual zone of residence (mobile or stationary), as well as engage in tasks such as cooking, cleaning and child caring. We might find domestic labour being performed, for example, in a supermarket, a community garden or a dumpster, as well as in streets, houses, units, caravans and tents.

Often, but not always, domestic labour is unpaid. While some of this labour is outsourced and distributed in the wider economy, blurring any boundaries between domestic and non-domestic, it would be a mistake to assume that the burden of domestic labour is necessarily lighter than in times past. Modernity's promise of reduced labour through increased technology and specialization in the industrial and post-industrial economy has not been fully realized. The sites and processes of mass consumption, including but not limited to domestic technologies such as washing machines and online shopping, do not necessarily – in and of themselves – lighten the load of domestic labour. Rather, they change its form, at times redistributing it; for example, from men to women. Domestic practices are now characterized by an abundance of choice and information; furthermore, that brings new analytical, administrative and organizational labours to the domestic space. This book is concerned with a wide variety of domestic work, but delimited by a particular moral investment in domestic labour that has emerged in association with modern environmentalism, broadly conceived. It is concerned with domestic environmental labour.

It is only recently, in the last few decades, that domestic space has become a focus for *personal* responsibilities for environmental care. While such personal responsibility, as I will explore, has received significant attention in some respects, and indeed has changed many domestic practices, only rarely has environmental care in domestic spaces been conceived as a form of labour. This book starts from the proposition that domestic labour, regardless of its form, has always shaped, and been shaped by, an elusive entity, perhaps best understood as having various guises. At least in Western contemporary discourse, which is the focus here, this entity is at times 'Nature', a mythical, sometimes mystical Other. It is also 'natural resources', conceived primarily in terms of its opportunities for human use. It is also 'the environment', a thing to be utilized and enjoyed yet respected and protected. *Domestic environmental labour*, however, is a phenomenon unique to the contemporary era. I will contend that domestic environmental labour is often carried out under the auspices of individualist and consumerist environmental politics. Thus, arguably new forms of environmental politics are embodied in household activities that ostensibly reduce impacts on Nature(s), but are often far removed from the households in question. Activities such as rinsing cans and sorting them into recycling receptacles, researching 'green' cleaning products or nappies, and installing and maintaining a set of solar panels are new types of domestic work that warrant examination. What is culturally and politically important about labour that is (typically) consciously undertaken for an entity named 'the environment'?

Domestic environmental labour, in an idealized form, involves accessing and using water to wash and bathe *without significant depletion or pollution of the water source*. It involves finding, nurturing, distributing, processing *and sustaining, over time*, plants and animals to eat, and materials to clothe, house, transport, entertain and keep cool or warm members of a household or commune. It involves keeping dirt at bay domestically without damaging non-domestic ecosystems, and sourcing *accessible and clean* energy for cooking, heating and cooling. It is with these types of domestic 'greening' activities that this book is chiefly concerned. For some who are socially as well as environmentally conscious, such labour needs to be undertaken *without reducing, and preferably advancing, others' (i.e. anyone beyond the confines of the domestic space in question) enjoyment of health, safety or financial well-being.* For some domestic environmental labourers, therefore, environmental concern is a primary driver. For others, both social and environmental concerns are important. There are, I contend, important social implications of domestic environmental labour either way. It is also my observation that domestic environmental labour is commonly mislabelled and misunderstood, and promoted and undertaken, euphemistically and optimistically, as good environmental (or social) practice or citizenship. In other words, putting out the recycling or installing a grey-water system can – politically – entail something more than a routinized expression of environmental care, and that this politics is not sufficiently taken into account. Domestic environmental labour is often labour-intensive, involving anything from sophisticated learning and creative effort, to mundane, repetitive, drudge-like chores, and it is implicated in wider social and political relations that are only beginning to be explored (Cox 2013; Gill *et al.* 2015; Marres 2011; Oates and McDonald 2006). My focus on domestic greening *as labour*, it should be noted, is a deliberate attempt to gain a better understanding of the broad realm of human activities often understood using the conceptual tools of ethical or green consumption, or environmental citizenship. And indeed, the first point of critique is to note that it is indeed a highly political maneouvre to isolate 'green consumption' or 'domestic greening' from the social milieu, potentially placing the environment in a hierarchical position above considerations of social equity. This is in part a historical legacy, but since it is now well accepted that the socio-environmental nexus needs to be understood as an interconnected system, any focus on environmental care over social care needs to be considered *as part of a politics of domestic environmental labour* in this knowledge context.

Domestic greening is defined here as the processes by which homes and domestic life are modified to include (ostensibly) more environmentally benign materials and activities. Placing work at the centre of analysis of domestic greening is necessary, I believe, to add freshness to understandings of domestic greening as deeply political. *Prima facie*, the moralizing link between domestic labour and environmental care makes some sense: why shouldn't we be *personally* responsible for our household interactions with Nature/resources/the environment, regardless of whether we characterize them as survival, consumption, citizenship, labour or something else? What are at stake here, however, are the social and material relations through which any care of ecological systems linked to domestic labour is achieved. Domestic activities do not connect with one, purified Nature – in a globalized world they connect with many natures, and simultaneously, many social groups, near and far. These interconnections are often so complex that they are almost impossible for ordinary citizens (and indeed experts as well) to materially, conceptually or politically disentangle. How is it possible to fully know the environmental and social impact of even a single consumption choice, or even to judge the relative impacts of two options? Outside debates about ethical consumption, furthermore, domestic connections with social groups are too frequently forgotten when domestic greening takes place. Individual–Nature relationships are typically prioritized. But precisely because of this often ignored or forgotten social complexity, whether or not domestic environmental labour advances social equity *and* environmental care is a big question, well worthy of attention from ecofeminist quarters. Here, the 'social' includes, but also goes beyond, the care of distant Others (e.g. through fair trade) implied in the term 'ethical consumption'. While of course much has already been achieved in this regard and this is hardly the first work to take an interest in either domestic greening, ethical consumption or domestic labour, I believe there remains new terrain to explore.

In this book I have the modest aim of *initiating* exploration of a simple but I believe powerful proposition, namely, that domestic labour consciously undertaken for an entity named 'the environment' is a phenomenon rarely acknowledged or debated – in policy, scholarship and everyday life. In this absence, there is a complex politics of gender, space, class and nature. The analytical absence of labour in many studies of greening activities and ethical consumption is not entirely surprising. As Uzzell and Räthzel (2013) point out, the construction of labour as nature's other has underscored a traditional antagonism between (formal) labour and environmental movements in the wider economy. Similarly, in research, labour has typically been neglected in environmental studies, while the environment is typically neglected in labour studies (Uzzell and Räthzel 2013). Betwixt these, however, a growing body of feminist and science and technology studies work that recognizes and attends to the contradictions, complexities and politics of 'green homemaking', and is highly instructive in understanding domestic environmental labour. This body of work has been influential in informing the discussions in this book (Cox 2013; MacGregor 2011; Marres 2011).

Domestic environmental labour, it will be argued, is under-valued in governance and the formal economy, much like other types of domestic labour, as long argued by feminists. In the interests of widespread voluntary uptake of domestic green activities, environmental policy typically does not position domestic greening as (often) low or unpaid, possibly dangerous and sometimes unsatisfying work. Householders engaged in domestic greening have become a largely unrecognized and unaccounted supply of green labour, a new version of domestic labour displaced from a visible to an invisible economy (Marres 2011). From a broadly feminist ecological citizenship viewpoint, which is where I position myself, any tendency to posit domestic greening as a gender neutral, practical form of environmental citizenship becomes a point of social critique, not a foundational assumption for improving ecological outcomes. It is clear that domestic environmental labour, along with other forms of domestic labour, is often feminized and undervalued. Since the home is traditionally feminized while the public sphere is masculinized, the 'domestication of greening' is another way in which care can be further privatized and feminized, possibly denying women's and non-Western cultural groups' equal participation in environmental citizenship:

> There are unfair gender asymmetries involved in greening the household, which stem from the traditional division of labour. … In so far as consumption is a private sphere activity, and women tend to be principally responsible for household consumption, it is likely that exhortations to 'live green' are directed at (and will be received primarily by) women. Men may hear them, but expect women to do the work. There is evidence to suggest that women are more likely than men to take on green housework.
>
> (MacGregor 2009, 134)

Indeed, the evidence is growing that women do much of the 'green housework', particularly the more mundane domestic greening tasks such as sorting the recycling (Oates and McDonald 2006; Organo *et al*. 2013). In a case study by Organo *et al*. (2013, 559), for example:

- Women 'spent more total time on sustainable practices, and did so more often. Men's contributions related mostly to gardening and transport, in longer blocks of time'.
- Women 'experienced time as overlapping and fragmented, with no distinction between work and leisure. Men contributed to sustainable practices mainly through activities understood as leisure, in longer blocks of time'.
- 'While men were often responsible for the labour and upfront time required to start or research a project, the responsibility of everyday implementation and habit-changing commonly fell to women.'

An ecofeminist critique of the dominant, ecological modernist environmental politics (which will be explored below) is that it pays insufficient attention to the politics of gender in general and the gendered division of labour in particular (MacGregor 2009). Feminist ecological citizenship sees care as a form of work and foregrounds the politicization of care as a necessary part of citizenship. It advances 'a positive political identity that allows women to express their gender-related concerns for environmental quality but that does not forever tie women (in general) to the private sphere of care and maternal virtue' (MacGregor 2011, 6–7). I agree with MacGregor (2011) that more traction can be gained from a theory of feminist ecological citizenship than from alternative ecofeminisms, particularly the ecomaternalisms which draw on the experience of women as mothers and care givers, as mediators of caring relationships between people and nature:

> Ecomaternalist arguments that celebrate women's caring for people and the planet without condemning its implication in oppressive political economic systems risk affirming sexist notions about women's place in society ... they are particularly dangerous in an era during which *unpaid caring work* is increasingly exploited to facilitate economic restructuring and the dismantling of the welfare state.
>
> (MacGregor 2011, 6–7; emphasis added)

The ecofeminism informing this book is one that conceptualizes domestic greening specifically as, often, unpaid caring work, but also more broadly considers Eurocentric mastery over women and nature as an interlinked phenomenon that needs unpacking at a variety of scales, including the domestic. In this book, I wish to consider conceptually the effects and implications of the *absence* of a concept of domestic environmental labour in the narratives that dominate much environmental social science scholarship and environmental policy, in Australia where I am based but also in the 'Global North' more broadly. I am interested in the politicized relations that shape, and are shaping of, ways in which householders work to successfully (or perhaps unsuccessfully) implement and use initiatives from eco-fashion to solar-powered hot water systems. If there is significant work involved in researching, evaluating, sourcing, selecting, designing, reusing, transporting, installing, modifying, maintaining, using, improving, upcycling, replacing and disposing of goods and services for reduced environmental impact in, of and around the home, there is a need to understand this work as a potential ramification of ecopaternalism and the greening of capitalism. There is also a need to consider how, if domestic environmental labour is undervalued and invisible, it might be better recognized (see also Glucksmann 2013). Ecofeminist studies have long engaged with questions of domestic labour and environmental citizenship of women, but such work has not significantly influenced the broad nexus of inter-disciplinary research into households and ecological impact. Indeed, the broader body of research is dominated by the concepts of environmental behaviour, practice theory and sustainable consumption theories. It is important, I believe, to do more ecofeminist research in this space.

This book speaks to these issues. Inspired in part by critical labour, environmental, and gender studies[1], but in essence it is none of these since it is a work of a cultural geographer. It is intended to be a popular cultural geography, more accessible than academic. I explore the proposition that the practice and politics of domestic labour being undertaken in the name of 'the environment' needs to be better recognized, understood and accounted for as a phenomenon shaped by, and shaping, social politics such as those of gender and class. Indeed, it may even be the case that domestic environmental labour needs to be better recognized, understood and accounted for by advocates of domestic greening before widespread domestic greening can take place. Such an approach may help to explain why a widespread transition to green homes has not materialized. I commence the task of understanding domestic environmental labour as a political activity by drawing on ideas about home, technology and nature in ecofeminism and cultural geography, attending to the contradiction between narratives of 'easy' greening on one hand, and the role played by householders as environmental labourers of different kinds on the other. Domestic environmental labour may, I argue, provide an alternative conceptual basis for understanding more deeply the possibilities and limitations of domestic greening. It is a concept that can shed new light on how domestic greening assists or detracts from the ways in which householders fashion themselves as environmentally responsible subjects.

Scope of the book

Although I have a personal concern for 'the environment' and hope that my own efforts, for example to limit consumption, save water and reduce waste at home, are somehow useful, to be clear I do not accept the normative positioning of domestic greening as possessing inherent moral worth. As such, it is not within the scope of this book to consider in any depth the extent to which particular domestic greening activities make a difference ecologically. Although I do not doubt that ecologically and socially beneficial consumption and domestic practices exist, I also believe that ecological (and sometimes labour-saving) benefits from green products and technologies are too frequently assumed, without sufficient consideration of the social and cultural context in which they are embedded. Thus, I approach domestic greening as a political and politicized human activity potentially shaped by, and shaping, social inequities.

It is also not within the scope of this book to consider the labour implications of 'greening' phenomena that are not primarily domestic. Those at a community, city or national scale, such as green urban development and green jobs in energy production are therefore not included in this work, except in a few ways that they link closely to the domestic, for example, tradespeople to whom domestic greening work, particularly those involving complicated technologies such as solar-panels, is sometimes outsourced. It should be noted, however, that any boundaries between the domestic and the non-domestic are fluid: they are not coterminous with the physical boundaries demarcating a place of residence, since people, energy, information and matter flow across such boundaries in all sorts of ways. Relatedly, attention to the social stratification and politics of the greening of public spaces is an important topic of research, as is that of environmental gentrification, green value-chains and so on, but these are not dealt with here. A further limitation is my focus on the developed world. There is a highly problematic narrative that positions developing world women as being 'closest to nature' and hence uncritically burdens this social group with more and more environmental work, both in and outside the home (Arora-Jonsson 2011; MacGregor 2009). This is a topic worthy of much critical attention, but is beyond the scope of this book.

The work is indirectly related to several years' empirical research investigating the challenges faced by householders in Australia (i.e. in a corner of the Global North) who are attempting to undertake green household activities[2] (Farbotko and Head 2013; Farbotko and Waitt 2011; Gibson *et al.* 2013; Head *et al.* 2013; Waitt *et al.* 2012). In this previous work, I conducted a series of interviews with householders in their homes discussing and observing the sometimes contested environmental and cultural impact of domestic greening activities. I explored the difficulties faced by householders in balancing domestic greening practices with other priorities such as family relations, budgets, health and comfort (e.g. Farbotko and Head 2013). During this fieldwork, I made an observation about domestic environmental labour – that it was largely absent from both everyday understandings of domestic greening as well as from the literature on environmental behavior, environmental practice and much of that in environmental citizenship. Intriguingly, the labour involved in domestic greening was making its presence known in sometimes significant ways and yet it was difficult to find the appropriate conceptual tools and resources with which to make sense of this domestic work. It was sometimes considered by research participants as highly burdensome and sometimes more positively experienced as a labour of love. I wondered what insights could be gained if labour was forefronted, instead of environmental behavior, values, or knowledge.

This book does not present new primary data on domestic environmental labour. While clearly an important limitation, the empirical project just discussed, which in part inspired this study, was not geared towards data generation for a rigorous empirical analysis of environmental labour. It is in fact beyond the ambitions of this small volume to commence what will hopefully be varied empirical explorations of domestic environmental labour, by myself and others, in the future. Making full sense of the gendered realities of domestic environmental labour is vitally important, but this requires detailed fieldwork which is well beyond the scope of this set of introductory and indeed only exploratory ideas. Here I only seek to make a contribution to an expanding discussion of domestic environmental labour by critical environmental social scientists, particularly ecofeminists and cultural geographers. My aim is to interpret a small selection of the diverse literature on domestic greening, forefronting the issue of domestic labour, while using case studies of particular domestic environmental labours to advance understanding of its politics. Hence, I draw on published primary and secondary materials to begin to explore the issues.

Chapter outline

This book is structured as follows. In Chapter 2, I look at the green home imperative, exploring the notion of home as a political and cultural, as much as a physical, space. This exploration sets the scene for a discussion of the domestication of greening, with 'greening' and 'home-making' considered as intertwined socio-political relations. I explore dominant domestic greening agendas and argue that little explicit acknowledgement of the labour involved in domestic greening is discernable. I centralize the observation that, in post-industrial Western societies in particular following the emergence of the global environmental crisis narrative in the twentieth century, domestic greening agendas positioned homes as suitable sites for specifically consumerist and technological responses to the global environmental crisis to be located. I consider ways in which much domestic greening rhetoric suggests *reduced* domestic labour through eco-efficient technology and green consumption, and posits an idealized domestic greener.

In Chapter 3, I consider some of the socio-political effects of domestic environmental labour as a largely *private* act. Since domestic greening is popularly and in policy ostensibly for *public* (environmental) good, it is worth examining some of the ways the private/public interface is negotiated here. I consider three types of domestic greening which arguably need to be understood in terms of the domestic *privatization of resources*: standalone houses versus unit blocks in Australia, 'off-gridding' and domestic water tank use. Standalone houses and unit blocks offer very different ways of expressing green politics at the domestic scale in Australia. 'Off-gridders' are a minority group at the more radical end of the domestic greening spectrum who choose to decouple as much as possible from centralized systems of provision of goods and services, such as water, food and electricity, in order to generate their own supply, often involving significant amounts of household labour. Urban domestic water tank use, on the other hand, has attained popular and political appeal in Australia where drought conditions in a changing climate are frequent, and water tanks are widely believed to 'save' water from centralized infrastructure. Despite their outwardly different resource politics, both water tank users and off-gridders engage in domestic environmental labour, I argue, largely in order to gain private control at the household scale over resource use, often for improved environmental outcomes, but not always *only* for improved environmental outcomes. In the case of urban domestic water tanks, the tank itself is delegated the task of 'saving water', and also becomes a culturally and politically powerful signifier of water conservation, whether or not decreases in consumption actually occur. In the remainder of Chapter 3, I consider how some domestic environmental labour is implicated in power relations extending well beyond the household. Separating household waste into recyclables for collection is widely practised even if the work involved is often conceived as simultaneously confusing and boring, and there is ambivalence about whether or not environmental benefits are resulting from this labour. The economic benefits accrued by waste management organizations from recycling voluntary labour are, intriguingly, rarely questioned: recyclers are essentially a zero-cost volunteer labour force for materials recovery enterprises, perhaps a successful instance of 'green capitalism'. Another case-study, of unskilled paid labourers being fatally injured on the job installing domestic insulation, provides an important warning of reliance on market-mechanisms to achieve domestic greening, and a grave reminder that social risks can never be ignored in the quest to make homes greener.

In Chapter 4, I explore how an alternative resource politics can emerge when domestic environmental labour disrupts, rather than accommodates or imitates, dominant market relations and intentionally seeks to enhance public goods in addition to private interests. Here I consider a case of refashioning used clothing as a form of labour-intensive domestic upcycling, that is simultaneously a political project extending well beyond the domestic space, through the use of social media. The chapter adopts a case-study approach, aiming to provide a detailed account of a new type of domestic environmental labour, namely, upcycle blogging, which is producing new forms of private–public space for resource politics.

The concluding chapter summarizes the key themes of the book, with suggestions for future research, particularly that which takes into account social relations not deeply explored in this introductory volume, such as ethnicity, age and ability, as well as the domestic environmental labour of low consumption households. For many committed environmentalists, the home will likely remain a key space in which to express and practice the version of environmental citizenship that makes the most sense to them, but neglecting the labour implications of this politics may be a fundamental barrier to achieving the deep economic, political, policy and institutional change likely to be required to truly achieve an equitable, and green, society.

Notes

1 This book does not seek to thoroughly canvass the literature on green labour, ecofeminism, ethical consumption or environmental behaviour, although elements of all these bodies of work have shaped its content and are cited accordingly.
2 I conducted the work as a Research Associate employed at the University of Wollongong under Australian Research Council (DP0986041) 'Making less space for carbon: cultural research for climate change mitigation and adaptation'.

References

Arora-Jonsson, S. (2011). Virtue and vulnerability: Discourses on women, gender and climate change. *Global Environmental Change*, 21(2), 744–751.

Cox, R. (2013). House/work: Home as a space of work and consumption. *Geography Compass*, 7(12), 821–831.

Farbotko, C., & Waitt, G. (2011). Residential air-conditioning and climate change: Voices of the vulnerable. *Health Promotion Journal of Australia: Official Journal of Australian Association of Health Promotion Professionals*, 22(Special Issue), S13.

Farbotko, C., & Head, L. (2013). Gifts, sustainable consumption and giving up green anxieties at Christmas. *Geoforum*, 50, 88–96.

Gibson, C., Farbotko, C., Gill, N., Head, L., & Waitt, G. (2013). *Household Sustainability: Challenges and Dilemmas in Everyday Life*. Cheltenham, UK: Edward Elgar Publishing.

Gill, N., Osman, P., Head, L., Voyer, M., Harada, T., Waitt, G., & Gibson, C. (2015). Looking beyond installation: Why households struggle to make the most of solar hot water systems. *Energy Policy*, 87, 83–94.

Glucksmann, M. (2013). Working to consume: Consumers as the missing link in the division of labour. Centre for Research in Economic Sociology and Innovation (CRESI), Working Paper 2013-03, University of Essex: Colchester.

Head, L., Farbotko, C., Gibson, C., Gill, N., & Waitt, G. (2013). Zones of friction, zones of traction: The connected household in climate change and sustainability policy. *Australasian Journal of Environmental Management*, 20(4), 351–362.

MacGregor, S. (2009). A stranger silence still: The need for feminist social research on climate change. *The Sociological Review*, 57(s2), 124–140.

MacGregor, S. (2011). *Beyond Mothering Earth: Ecological Citizenship and the Politics of Care*. Vancouver: UBC Press.

Marres, N. (2011). The costs of public involvement: Everyday devices of carbon accounting and the materialization of participation. *Economy and Society*, 40(4), 510–533.

Oates, C. J., & McDonald, S. (2006). Recycling and the domestic division of labour: Is green pink or blue?. *Sociology*, 40(3), 417–433.

Organo, V., Head, L., & Waitt, G. (2013). Who does the work in sustainable households? A time and gender analysis in New South Wales, Australia. *Gender, Place & Culture*, 20(5), 559–577.

Uzzell, D., & N. Räthzel (2013). Mending the breach between labour and nature: A case for environmental labour studies. In: *Trade Unions in the Green Economy: Working for the Environment*. London: Routledge.

Waitt, G., Caputi, P., Gibson, C., Farbotko, C., Head, L., Gill, N., & Stanes, E. (2012). Sustainable household capability: Which households are doing the work of environmental sustainability?. *Australian Geographer*, 43(1), 51–74.

2 The green home imperative

Homemaking

Kaika (2004) explains how dwellings become homes when they are imbued with cultural and ideological meanings. Modern homes are very different, for instance from the more communally oriented dwellings of many indigenous societies:

> The bourgeois home operates as a blissful private shelter insofar as it is selectively sealed from the world outside. One can be lost forever inside one's own painstakingly created familiarity, insofar as one is confined inside it. By eliminating (visually, perceptually and discursively-ideologically) the material connections and social relations that make its existence possible, the modern 'home' acquires the properties of both a refuge and a prison.
>
> (Kaika 2004, 279)

The Enlightenment attempted to position homes as apolitical spaces, providing the white western male subject with the promise of a private space in which individual freedom could be enjoyed and undesirables – both social and natural – could be excluded (Kaika 2004). A great deal of energy continues to be invested in furthering the Enlightenment's ideal of domestic space, particularly through the performance of dual domestic and public spheres. The idealized, liberal fiction of a safe, private, apolitical house persists in the Western imagination and in the cultural economy. Yet such a fiction can only be sustained with reference to a binary other. The creation of an Australian modernity, for example, has been argued to rely on the ability of a majority to shuttle back and forth between a (masculinized) modern world ruled by dispassionate reason and efficient technology and a (feminized) domestic idyll characterized by sentiment, tradition, religion and nature (Davison 2011, 43). Home is 'a state of being' and, despite the

Enlightenment's privacy ideal, is 'not a static entity with clear boundaries but involves dynamic interconnections between inside and outside and private and public' (Bhatti and Church 2001, 369). Capitalism has rendered the *market value* of the home greatly significant. Modern homes are, complexly, financial assets or liabilities as well as physical and emotional space. For those who consider their homes as suitable sites to locate an environmental politics, moreover, the complexity is only compounded, as tradeoffs are made between pressures to be green, financially wise, comfortable, safe, relaxed and private (Head and Gibson 2012).

Attempting to work towards an idealized home which actively excludes unwelcome others and natures through its material 'completeness' is always an incomplete project. Interactions between dwellers and natures vary; and are mediated by the social and policy context in which homes are made. The home is not necessarily synonymous with a physical dwelling, but can spill over into outside space, and for some, not just in terms of the private yard or garden, but into public landscapes and of course, resource infrastructures (Reid and Beilin 2015). Nature can also 'unmake' homes, during times of disaster for example, but this is likely to be an uneven experience. For example Lesbian, Gay, Bisexual and Transsexual households are not necessarily factored into the heteronormativity of disaster policies (Gorman-Murray *et al.* 2014).

Domestic spaces are thus exceedingly complex, but also ambiguous, and non-static (Blunt 2005). They are interconnected rather than holistically private, possibly dangerous rather than inherently comfortable, and always fundamentally political (Brickell 2012). While often aspired to, and sometimes experienced in terms of comfort, cleanliness and convenience (Shove 2003) or resistance to unwelcome external (e.g. racialized) politics (hooks 1990) they can just as easily be sites of violence, economic anxiety, environmental and industrial risk, and social isolation. From domestic violence, to exposure to asbestos and mould, to mortgage stress and heat stress (Allon 2008; Houston and Ruming 2014; Mee *et al.* 2014; Warrington 2001), homes can be sites where emotional and physical well-being is damaged rather than nurtured. In times of risk, one's commitment to 'defending' home (for example, in the face of bushfire) can be lethal. So too can lack of social support exacerbated by the privileging of the privacy of home (Klinenberg 2015; Reid and Beilen 2015; Warrington 2001). Furthermore, perhaps counter-intuitively, technological 'solutions' that assume a private home *can* be technologically shielded against an external risk might amplify overall vulnerability. Air-conditioning use in private homes during heat waves, for example, can exacerbate rather than reduce the risk of heat stress through contributing to regional power-outs (Farbotko and Waitt 2011).

The making of 'home' as a private, safe, comfortable space in response to and yet also in defiance of risk is an ongoing endeavor, never actually complete, intertwined with social and cultural identities – including aspirations to live more greenly and associated practices. Home-making involves ongoing political and symbolic work: efforts to achieve homes as some combination of green, private, safe, stylish, comfortable, autonomous, wise investments involve a complex cultural politics. For modern households, particularly in the minority Global North, consumption defines a certain normality of home: making spaces that 'feel homelike' typically involves consumption thinking (Cox 2013). It is not surprising, therefore, that domestic greening is often imagined in ways that interlock with both modern 'comfort' thinking and consumption. Furthermore, consumption involves work (Glucksmann 2013). 'Consumption at home creates work and is a form of work itself. Few activities in the home are separable from the work that goes on there, and consumption is intimately tied to domestic labour' (Cox 2013, 821). As Cox (2013, 828) explains further, 'although consumption may seem like a form of leisure – the opposite of work – the two activities are, in fact, often indivisible. We rely on consumer goods to carry out housework, and our purchasing of things for our homes creates work, for ourselves and sometimes others.' The politics of home is also continually remade and reshaped in relation to the changing non-domestic: the politics and practices of resource provision are in flux. Thus the home, and the householder, connect with changing broader politics of provision. Residential premises, for instance, were once primarily conceived simply as end-of-pipe destinations for centralized, state-owned water and power infrastructure. In a context of increasing deregulation and privatization of public utilities, however, homes are being re-imagined as appropriate sites for water and solar power collection and storage through the use of domestic rainwater tanks and solar panels. These are typically understood as resource 'saving' or 'green' technologies. It is in such a broad sense that I consider 'home' in this work as a space of continual negotiation and tension between consumption and production, leisure and labour, autonomy and connection, comfort and risk: there are no fixed categories here.

Domestic greening can only be fully understood in terms of changing meanings, experiences and practices of 'home' in higher-income societies (see Allon 2008; Davison 2011). High consumption households are less likely to see their dwellings and outdoor spaces as sites of continuous work and more as, ideally, objects to be admired, used and enjoyed perhaps after a period of intensive renovating and decorating labour (Bhatti and Church 2001). There is an idealized 'finished' home that is longed for, although perhaps rarely achieved in practice, as there is always the mundane task of maintenance (Graham and Thrift 2007). Here, home is necessarily an ongoing process but the dream of a finished home – the perfect space of leisure – remains, particularly in consumerist narratives. For example:

There is growing evidence that the idea of low maintenance or 'minimum' garden is taking over encouraged by the garden industry and changing leisure and consumption habits. Increasingly, the front garden is hard standing for the car, and the back a private outdoor 'living room', lawned and part 'patioed' for ease of use and easy care. This shift from a cultivation-based gardening to home-based leisure use is accompanied by a desire to keep effort and time for maintenance to a minimum.

(Bhatti and Church 2001, 371)

Thus, we see how the home becomes a site where human-nature relations are re-imagined, in an unfolding and shifting series of relations between householders and the broader political, economic and cultural systems to which they are materially and symbolically connected.

Green capitalism – setting the scene

Situating domestic greening within the political economy is important:

For most people in the minority world, our lives are inextricably tied to capitalist forms of production and exchange, even as we go about cooking, cleaning and caring for loved ones – activities that so often appear to be outside the relations of paid work and consumption. These intimate, home-based activities are networked to the wider world, through flows of goods, the international migrations of domestic workers and our attempts to protect the environment as we consume more sustainably.

(Cox 2013, 828)

Businesses attempting to tap into, nurture, and often, profit from, the emergent 'green consumer' must be considered as part of the politics of domestic greening, as must governments, which are often concerned with promoting domestic greening through markets. However, domestic greening agendas have been often critiqued for a myopic focus, a failure to recognize larger scale power relations contributing to environmental and social impact (Marres 2008; Potter and Oster 2008).

Global systems of provision, green or otherwise, are mostly characterized by capitalism, the economic system of production and exchange based on the production of goods and services for sale. One enduring way of understanding the dynamics of this system is to explore the roles of two different classes: that of capital, and that of labour. According to Marx, labour as a class is a collective term for the segment of the population dependent on paid work to earn their living. Because members of this class do not own means of production (land, factories, resources, infrastructure, i.e. the factors of production other than labour), they are obliged to sell their labour power (ability to do work that contributes to the production of a good or service for sale) to the capitalist class. Labour as a class thus can be understood in relation to a capitalist class, i.e. those who collectively own the means of production (Deutz 2014). Bringing labour into visibility is important in environmental studies, according to O'Connor (1994) because it complicates relationships between capital and nature that are often imagined to exist along a linear continuum: from remaking capital in ways that are consistent with sustainability of nature, to remaking of nature by capital into its own image. Labour adds a third dimension, aiding understanding of the relationship between capital and nature, and the domestic scale is no exception.

How does labour complicate the relationship between nature and capital? In the formal economy, for the capitalist class who are most fundamentally concerned with generating a financial profit either directly from nature or indirectly, workers are a cost that needs to be minimized. But there is a contradiction in capitalism when one considers the overlap between labour and market. Capitalism, to succeed, typically needs to keep wages low, while having a populace with sufficient spending power to provide a market for the goods they have helped to produce (Deutz 2014). One way for this to happen is through the production of low-quality goods in places where workers are not well-protected by legislation or unions, combined with global trade opportunities. The result is a large market for cheap products with cheap wage costs, and negative social impacts on workers. At this end of the spectrum, sustainable use of nature is usually of very limited concern to producers. Another way to reduce costs, however, is to use more efficient or innovative technology to reduce resources used in production: more sustainable uses of nature here can be either recognized or unrecognized side effects of production. An alternative way to increase profits is to use marketing techniques to create demand for a more expensive or new product. There are myriad ways that the marketing world does this, but for green products, marketing can take the form of tapping into a political concern among consumers for protecting nature or the environment, in order to sell products that are either more sustainably produced or appear to be more sustainably produced, even if they are not. This ostensibly 'green' corner of the capitalist economy has arguably enrolled 'green consumers' as a very cost-effective, but largely unrecognized, voluntary labour force. Those consumers concerned with greening their homes and lifestyles are undertaking some of green capital's labour voluntarily – ostensibly for the environment, but also, within a capitalist system, necessarily to increase profits in the capitalist class. Householders thus become an unrecognized and unaccounted supply of labour for the greening of capitalism, labour which is under-valued in governance and the formal economy, much like other types of domestic labour. It is important to note at this point that only very small portions of the global economy purport to be 'green'. Nevertheless, this labour is of considerable interest because it can contribute to an understanding of the possibilities for, and limits to, the fostering of domestic greening by green capitalism. As will be discussed in Chapter 3, for example, unpaid or low-paid and unskilled labourers who are being outsourced to undertake some of the work of domestic greening can be at considerable risk in a system dominated by capitalist logics, particularly when regulation of safety and health risks of emergent green technologies is absent.

A significant issue with the green capitalist path to domestic greening is that often, consumption itself is not reduced. Technologist 'solutions' are often implemented through new forms of consumption. A focus on recycling, furthermore, does little to curb the generation of excess in the first place. Technologies have inefficiencies. For example, solar hot water systems can have structural leaks that are difficult to fix and result in increasing consumption of water (Gill *et al.* 2015). Green marketing can be more concerned with the appearance than with the actualization of reduced ecological impact. Volkswagen is one multinational company exposed for making false claims about reduced ecological impact, doctoring the engines of its supposedly low-emissions vehicles to produce false results on emission tests (Krall and Peng 2015). When green marketing claims are unfounded, feelings of responsibility – or even guilt about resource-intensive 'lifestyles'– are co-opted for capitalist accumulation purposes, sidelining actual reductions in environmental and social impact (Smerecnik and Renegar 2010). When such green washing is exposed, more credible business within the green economy can be damaged. With trust eroded, other more genuinely 'green' products may be dismissed by increasingly cynical consumers. Other contradictions emerge too to generate cynicism: consumers might be advised to 'save money and the environment' by energy companies. A consumer would be correct to wonder how committed a for-profit electricity company might be to achieving decreased demand for energy by the consumers who buy their product, particularly when supply expansion is being simultaneously planned in a for-profit enterprise. 'Green washing' was a major concern amongst all women in Organo *et al.*'s (2013) study of domestic greening. Each female participant expressed their frustration with flawed advertising which claimed that a product was environmentally friendlier than its competitors and spent considerable time (and effort) researching sustainable products in order to avoid green washing.

It is not only 'green' businesses deriving benefits from the purported greening of capitalism. With a trend towards an increasing gap between rich and poor globally, and at the level of the nation-state, it is not trite to observe that while the rich can purchase and benefit from green products – from organic produce to green building consultants – the poor can struggle to access even basic needs such as waste collection services, food security and clean water. The public/private divide is important here, with the rich able to privately enjoy the fruits of (often purchased) environmental activities, and the poor more likely to be exposed to risks arising from poor management of private resources and the commons more broadly. If public (including environmental) goods are to be better managed and more equitably enjoyed through individual and household choices about resource use, which surely is a basic premise of domestic greening, it is important to trace the uneven distribution of social 'goods' and 'bads' that might be furthered when domestic greening takes place. For example, across Australia, water is being reconceptualized from a public to a private asset by state and private enterprise, but (as will be discussed in detail in the next chapter) this has material and financial implications for the ways in which households imagine and use their water; many wealthier households now benefit from 'luxury' tank water and yet all households are now facing higher water bills (Farbotko *et al.* 2014). It is important to consider the inequitable distributions of benefits of domestic greening activities within green capitalism, and the ways in which power relations sustaining these inequitable distributions are reproduced or perhaps challenged.

Interestingly, despite such concerns, 'the formidable support for capitalistic agency as the primary means for social [including green] issue engagement' remains, and yet this 'significantly limits the populace from conceptualizing and engaging in other alternatives to creating a more sustainable future' (Smerecnik and Renegar 2010, 166). Technical innovation and reduced ecological impact are assumed to be optimized by capitalist markets, along with profit, with environmentally minded green consumers driving demand for green products. There is a widespread belief that growth in the purportedly green economy is desirable. However, the green economy is supported not just by 'consumers' but also by domestic environmental labour, which is central to new understandings of a somewhat internally contradictory politics of domestic resource use, as will be explored.

Domesticating greening: the home as site of environmental concern

Barr *et al.* (2011, 1243) write that, 'in both policy and academic writings, the home environment has been widely used as the default framing device for debates concerning sustainable lifestyles.' When sustainability emerged as a contested but nevertheless widely articulated global ideal in the late twentieth century, high-consuming households were addressed as bearers of significant 'green' responsibilities (Barr *et al.* 2011; Hobson 2002; Potter and Oster 2008). According to Barr *et al.* (2011, 1225), 'citizen–consumers [were] as critical to the neo-liberal state's governance of environmental issues as state or corporate actors.' Homes were simultaneously imagined as suitable sites for individual responses to the global environmental crisis to be located; political change was imagined as best effected through consumer activity, in material rather than discursive or philosophical ways. Buoying this continuing agenda is a belief that, with the correct information and technological advancement, along with an appropriate amount of 'behaviour change', perhaps helped along with financial subsidies, ecological benefits will accrue from green consumption and associated domestic greening practices, and that they are, therefore, morally worthwhile activities (Adams and Raisborough 2010). Interestingly, the imperative to green the home has been stronger than a broader project of greening 'lifestyles'. There is empirical evidence, for example, that individuals are more likely to engage in greening activities at home than elsewhere. Being green at home does not necessarily translate into green leisure and travel activities (Barr *et al.* 2011). Further, being green at home does not necessarily translate into engagement in more expansive forms of green politics. For example, householders who have implemented domestic greening activities, such as growing vegetables and sharing bath water among family members, do not necessarily engage in the giving of 'green gifts' at Christmas to extended family members (Farbotko and Head 2013). In that study, those committed to domestic greening believed that social bonds, between extended family members were strengthened through 'regular' gift giving. However, 'green gifts' were seen as potentially a weakening force, working against these bonds. Domestic greening practices were certainly seen as desirable among domestic greeners, but this was limited to the nuclear family, and only outside the festive season. Children of domestic greener parents, typically, were strongly encouraged to engage in water saving and growing vegetables and so on throughout the year. But the same children did not receive green gifts from their parents at Christmas. Only in rare cases were they given a reduced number of gifts. Within the (non-festive) domestic space, the choice to engage in domestic greening was imagined as largely apolitical or politically benign, apparently supported by the liberal ideology of individual choice. However, green gifts were deemed to be 'too political' for the festive season (Farbotko and Head 2013).

Indeed, it is worth pointing out that domestic greening is often constructed as *apolitical*, a matter for Policy not political debate. For ecofeminists, however, any resource use has a politics, and the home is always political space. When constructed as apolitical, particular types of domestic greening activities can become normalized, and remain largely beyond critique. A very significant politics of domestic resource privatization becomes apparent when domestic greening activities are analyzed as labour, as we shall see in later chapters. For now, it is worth bringing into visibility the often hidden politics of the liberal idealized home, with a good resale potential, which looms large in the project of domestic greening; a space in which to financially invest for the future and perhaps implement practices of 'green home-making' that are, ostensibly, at once cost-effective and environmentally friendly. Thus, a domestic greener may consider the installation of a water tank and solar panels as beneficial in multiple ways, offering not only a reduction in household environmental impact, but adding financial value to the home and possibly reducing utility bills. These choices shape resource politics in many ways. For example, an insidious politics of domestic greening emerges in the ideology of the liberal home; it is important, and far from apolitical, that the home is widely accepted to be a space of individual freedom, including the freedom to exclude undesirables. Freedom to exclude has a converse, namely, an assumed freedom to use privately those resources collected within the private space, such as rainwater collected in tanks. Another aspect of the politics of the green liberal home is that, like modern homes more generally, they are idealized (and marketed) primarily as sites of leisure rather than work. It is thus not surprising to find green policy prioritizing messages of 'ease' and 'simplicity'; presumably these appeal more to most householders being urged to voluntarily be more green at home than messages of 'hard work':

> The new challenge is to use our technology to minimize environmental impact while continuing to improve the comfort and performance of the homes we create.
>
> (Australian Government publication – Your Home: Australia's guide to environmentally sustainable homes)[1]

In this particular government promotion of domestic greening, labour is glossed as a 'new challenge' and home-making is a 'creative' act. The emphasis is on making homes (and not, importantly, householders) better 'performers', of both greening and comfort. Technology, not people, is expected to do most of the work. Such leanings towards technological determinism, in science and technology studies, is deserving of critical analysis (Flichy 2007). Similarly, a focus here is on creativity, aesthetics and 'practical' information rather than work *per se*:

> At Sanctuary we aim to bring you fresh inspiration and practical info and advice to help you beautify your home and lighten its environmental footprint.
>
> (Sanctuary: Modern Green Homes – 'the best green shelter magazine available anywhere')[2]

These types of imaginings of the green home occur within a populist ecological modernization discourse, dovetailing with green capitalist values, in which technical innovation and reduced environmental impact are assumed to be optimized by the open market, with little government intervention beyond 'education' and financial subsidies. This is the dominant agenda for domestic greening, prioritizing consumerist and technologist domestic greening activities, such as government incentives for domestic insulation and solar panel installations; invigoration of household water tank installation and use as ecologically worthwhile; household waste separation into recyclables and non-recyclables for collection and processing by local waste recovery operations, often for profit; growth in availability of a range of shopping receptacles that purport to be less resource intensive than the disposable plastic bag; and marketing of ostensibly green products, from jeans to toilet paper to cars. This dominant version of domestic greening, ecologically modernist in flavor, seems to promise both a smaller household ecological footprint and, importantly, implies reduced domestic labour through eco-efficient technology and green consumption (Davison 2011; Marres 2011). According to the populist ecological modernist discourse, what householders need to do to green their homes and their lifestyles is to shop for innovative green and eco-efficient products, tasks that ostensibly involve minimal effort.

The promise of reduced labour: the dominant greening agenda

Marres describes how the codification of domestic appliances in terms of their capacity to 'make things easy' contributes to the framing of domestic life as a private sphere of leisure, set against the professional sphere of work:

> Invocations of the idea that things must be 'made easy' for everyday subjects have particular normative implications, including the bifurcation of two domains of engagement with public affairs – one for professionals and one for laypeople, one for insiders and one for outsiders … [do] devices that are framed as turning environmental engagement into something 'easy' or 'fun' contribute to a similar bifurcation of the public and a related displacement of labour?
>
> (Marres 2011, 518–519)

Marres' work considers anew the feminist critique of technology that insists there is deception involved when technology in the home is categorized as easy and/or fun. Such a deception facilitates a displacement of labour from a visible to an invisible economy:

The trope of 'making things easy' has figured prominently in the history of domestic technology. As feminist studies of the 'industrial revolution in the home' have famously argued, the introduction of modern domestic appliances at the turn of the twentieth century was accompanied by a distinctive ideological theme: the idea that technology 'saves labour' … The introduction of modern appliances like electric stoves, vacuum-cleaners and refrigerators into middle-class households was legitimated in terms of the capacity of these technologies to 'make things easy' for modern housewives. It thus seems no coincidence that current attempts to 'environmentalize' households – or even society as a whole – would deploy these same domestic technologies and evoke the same capacity for saving labour and making things easy.

(Marres 2011, 518)

The dominant agenda for domestic greening, which positions much domestic greening on a one-dimensional political axis of ecological modernization, has little to gain by environmental 'practices' understood as being labour-intensive, particularly those that involve a significant level of drudgery. Domestic greening is almost reified, in some policy and research arenas, for its capacity to let everyone easily do their bit for the environment. Domestic greeners are imagined to need large helpings of ease, comfort, beauty and leisure if the environmental impact of homes is to be reduced through their domestic activities. The role of householders in the ecological modernization project is simplified, as end-users of the goods and services of green production. According to the ecological modernist discourse, minimal effort is required for householders to do their bit to protect the environment, as greening homes and lifestyles involves mainly shopping for innovative green and eco-efficient products. The slogan of Greenhome.com captures this message succinctly: 'shop green, live green'. A campaign in Australia titled 'Sustainability begins at home' encourages households to become greener by promising that activities associated with this endeavor would take little time, be easy to do, and result in positive feelings:

No matter where you're at, [you can] take the challenge to see just how easy it is to take control of your ecological footprint. You'll be surprised how little time it takes to make a difference …. and how good it makes you feel!

(Sustainable Illawarra 2008, cited in Organo *et al.* 2013, 560)

In parallel to the rise of consumption as a primary vehicle for cultural identity, not only in domestic greening but in modern life more generally, Marres notes that participation in public affairs, environmental or otherwise, is now conceptualized as something that must somehow be made 'doable' for everyday people – who lack the time, space and shared knowledge that political engagement requires (Marres 2011, 517). The 'ease of green shopping' message fits with wider aspirational, consumerist lifestyles characterized by a perceived dislocation from civic life and a retreat to the shelter of private life (Craig 2010).

Environmental citizenship, when imagined in consumption terms, can appear to justify the transferral of costs for transition to a sustainable economy to 'green consumers' (Slocum 2004; Hinchcliffe 1996). But green consumers are also mythologized as passive subjects existing in an (ultimately fictional) leisurely realm of consumer choice. As green consumers, householders are not only being addressed as bearing a significant portion of responsibility for greening by absorbing the costs of the green economy, but the labour associated with this responsibility is being made invisible by the myth of the leisure of consumer choice combined with technological advances in green products. Furthermore, the technologies through which domestic greening are to be achieved are typically welcomed into the domestic space based on *their assumed capacity to do a lot of the work of greening for us* (Marres 2011). Green products are imagined to do certain tasks, to actually achieve a good portion of the effort needed to help reduce environmental impact in everyday life. Thus, it is energy efficient light bulbs that are imagined to 'save electricity'. Water tanks, to take another example, collect and store water, ostensibly freeing up householders to do other things, while the actual green task of 'saving water' is imagined to be achieved by the tank itself.

The green consumer is thus mythologized as a largely passive, yet rational being; green consumption decisions are assumed to be made on the basis of an imaginary easy access to good quality information, in a leisurely realm of (rational) consumer choice and voluntary green cost-benefit decision-making (e.g. Gill *et al.* 2015). The now well-accepted household greening activities such as installing water tanks and buying green cleaning products are being normatively positioned as inherently labour-light, consumption based and morally and ecologically worthwhile. As a result, domestic environmental labour is in danger of remaining poorly understood. Yet, it is interesting and important to note that efforts involved in becoming green at home have been far from minimal (Gibson *et al.* 2013; Gill *et al.* 2015; Vannini and Taggart 2016). Further, while the ecological modernist agenda for domestic greening suggests a technologically driven easy transition to green homes, such a transformation has not materialized in any widespread way (Davison 2011).

Why then, is domestic greening still so important on policy agendas and, on the other hand, why is the promise of easy domestic greening not being interrogated more deeply? An important issue that is rarely discussed is that technologies through which domestic greening are to be achieved have often been promoted and adopted in such terms without sufficient regard to the associated risks: their perceived green and labour saving benefits seem to outweigh health, social and environmental risks, which are sometimes significant. Suburban water tank owners, for instance, are often not aware, or not concerned about, the public health dangers of their tanks. However, they are typically deeply familiar with, and accepting of, the discourse that tanks are 'water-saving devices'. The point is that such green technologies are usually positioned in policy and public discourse as socially benign, at least until revealed otherwise (e.g. Parker 2013).

Thus, as Marres notes, 'we begin to see how eco-homes [and perhaps green technologies more broadly] might produce asymmetries between those domestic subjects who have successfully delegated their civic duties [to the environment] to their newly acquired or retrofitted houses, and those who are burdened by unfulfillable responsibilities vis-a-vis the environment' (2008, 39). In other words, there are myriad possibilities for rich households to purchase an ecological modernist version of environmental citizenship by acquiring sophisticated 'green' technologies that may have unrecognized social risks, while those who cannot afford to do so might be left with more labour-intensive forms of environmental citizenship, whether material or political.

Green consumption work

As discussed above, supply–demand relationships of domestic greening are shaped by green capitalism, a political economy in which a new market around 'easy greening' has emerged, but which has also shifted some of the cost of both real greening and greenwash to the voluntary labour force provided by householders keen to lower their environmental impact by greening their homes. Householders are increasingly faced with the paradox that achieving the 'easy green' lifestyle turns out to mean significant input of largely unacknowledged domestic environmental labour. As consumers confront the day-to-day burdens associated with this unexpected work, there is considerable space for apathy and disengagement with green politics to set in.

There is value at this point to considering 'consumption work' in more detail:

> Housework and consumption have often been regarded as binary opposites, and research has tended to see its focus as on one or the other. Consumption is generally thought of as a leisure activity, a form of relaxation and the opposite of work: it might be a browse in the shopping centre, a self-indulgent meal or a holiday in the sun. However, … consumption is also closely bound up with necessary activities and

work, particularly in the home .... Refocusing on the work of consumption allows for a broader understanding of both activities.

(Cox 2013, 821)

Consumption work determines what is actually consumed. Different people may acquire the same goods but what they consume will differ depending on the consumption work expended on them. What is bought does not determine what is consumed, and consumption work represents a key bridging activity between acts of purchase and acts of consumption.

(Glucksmann 2013, 14–15)

If 'consumption-work' sounds like an oxymoron, this is precisely the point. Few goods or services, green or otherwise, are delivered 'complete' to consumers in the sense of being ready for use without further activity. Yet the role of consumers in completing a system of provision with their own labour is not often acknowledged in theories of either work or consumption. Recognition of the interdependence between work undertaken prior to and after the purchase of goods and services problematizes any assumption that only post-purchase activity comprises consumption. Further, it calls for a conception of the division of labour that extends from the market and world of paid employment to also encompass the usually unpaid labour of the end user. Consumption work is defined as 'all work undertaken by consumers necessary for the purchase, use, re-use and disposal of consumption goods' (Glucksmann 2013, 2).

Cox (2013) agrees that is important to reveal consumption as being inseparable from work in the home as this disrupts the casual dualisms of public/private, work/home and production/consumption, which are strongly gendered. The extent of home-making work, Cox argues, should be revealed as part of an ongoing project to expose the amount of women's unpaid work and the value and variety of reproductive labour (Cox 2013). Is domestic greening, then, part of an ongoing manipulation of women as 'home-makers' tasked by a patriarchal society with finding a meaningful existence in making the perfect home through [ethical] consumption (Cox 2013)? The consumption involved in home-making can be both drudge-like and highly meaningful, but either way it involves work that is under-valued and unrecognized in comparison to paid labour. The work of home-based consumption is an acceleration of promises of labour-saving technology that result in new forms of work and new divisions of labour (Cox 2013). For example:

Piped water reduced the considerable labour of carrying water and slops but it also raised standards of cleanliness and underpinned the consumption of cleaning products and use of appliances. Often, the task that was carried out had been carried out by men, whereas those that grew were carried out by women.

(Cox 2013, 823)

Domestic environmental labour is no exception. Cox (2013, 828) goes on:

> Research on work and consumption in the home has diversified considerably since the secondwave feminists raised the issue of women's unequal burden of domestic responsibility and showed that the work that goes on in the home is real work. Housework has long been tied to consumption, and we are increasingly aware of the complexities of this relationship, its geographic and historical specificities and how the physical nature of housing and domestic technologies create the need for different forms of consumption while networking the home to global economic and environmental processes.

Mass-produced home cleaning products still need labour; cooking may be either a burden or a source of leisure, but perhaps most frequently, a combination of the two (Cox 2013). For householders attempting to be 'green', consumption work often involves the task of ensuring and evaluating improved environmental outcomes, even when faced with uncertainty or inconsistency. Whether or not lay evaluations accord with reduced environmental impact is often unclear and indeed, almost unmeasurable, but such evaluations are constantly being undertaken. For example, in Sweden, consumers make trips to recycling stations and evaluate these trips according to the potential gains consumers perceive such trips bring to the environment. Making special trips is perceived to undermine the environmental benefit of recycling and so sending the waste to incineration is viewed as a better option than making a special trip (Wheeler and Glucksmann 2015).

When complex domestic greening technologies are involved in 'green consumption', and yet suppliers are mostly focused on sale and installation rather than ongoing maintenance and use, improved environmental outcomes may be less likely than technological hassles with maintenance, which is work (Gill *et al.* 2015). Gill *et al.* (2015) studied users of solar hot water systems, dividing them into two types: active and passive. The active users made reference to the considerable work involved in managing and monitoring system use, and yet the work put in mostly did not result in a satisfactory system. These active users were typically 'highly-educated and informed individuals who were nonetheless confounded by the level of complexity involved in choosing, installing and operating the systems as well as the multiple types of rebates and regulatory incentives involved in the process' (Gill *et al.* 2015, 88). Gill *et al.* (2015) found an explicit frustration among solar hot water users – that there was no easy path to reduced consumption and acceptable access to hot water delivered by this technology. Nevertheless, these consumers retained a focus on 'technical adjustments to the operation of the system rather than behaviour modification' such as changing the timing of showers (Gill *et al.* 2015, 90). Gill *et al.*'s (2015) study demonstrates Glucksmann's (2013, 14–15) contention that 'consumption work determines what is actually consumed. Different people may acquire the same goods but what they consume will differ depending on the consumption work expended on them. What is bought does not determine what is consumed, and consumption work represents a key bridging activity between acts of purchase and acts of consumption.' Following on, the purchase of domestic greening products is typically understood to result in reduced consumption, but this is an assumption that is ripe for reconsideration, using the concept of domestic environmental labour.

Idealized domestic greener

According to research in the academic discipline of environmental psychology, a person is likely to be concerned about the environment and act on its behalf if:

> they have spent time in nature as a child; if they possess accurate knowledge of the environment, its problems and potential solutions; if they have an open, agreeable and conscientious personality; if they consider the future consequences of their actions; if they feel in control of their behaviours; if they harbor biospheric, post-material, liberal values and responsibility for environmental problems; if they are among the upper half of the economic classes; if they hold personal and descriptive norms about pro-environmental action; if they adhere to a religion that teaches a stewardship orientation to the earth; and if they spend time in non-consumptive nature activities.
>
> (Gifford and Nilsson 2014, 151)

This review of the state of knowledge in environmental psychology contains no explicit acknowledgement or evaluation of an individual's attitude to or social characteristics as a domestic labourer or indeed in terms of labour of any sort. Nor does it situate the individual within systems of resource use. The only evidence of the political economy is rather troubling from a perspective of social equity; that it is those who already have greater access to and control of resources that are likely to do anything about environmental problems. While in one sense it is ethically correct to apply the 'polluter pays' principle here and accept that the upper half of the economic classes *should* shoulder the burden of rectifying environmental problems, there is a risk here too. Those who have the time and resources to devote to environmental concern and action because of their privileged position in society are likely to countenance 'solutions' that do not threaten that privilege, including the right to continue to control and use resources to maintain the particular way of living that they believe is comfortable and acceptable. Advocates (from any social group) of a *less* comfortable standard of living are exceedingly rare. Moreover, the absence of labour in the above-quoted analysis is widely observable across the environmental social sciences, and it is precisely this absence that enables some of the privileges of the 'green elite' to be reproduced. In tasking everyone to do their bit, important patterns of unevenness in domestic greening, work and wealth in ecological modernization discourse become downplayed. Indeed, the practice of the populist version of ecological modernization ideology often requires both financial capital and a feeling of green responsibility among its consumers but 'the work of being sustainable' is a burden that is not shared equally between or within households. Women, for example, do more of the work of sustainable consumption and have higher expectations of what should be carried out, and this is linked to the traditional gendered division of labour within the home (Cox 2013).

While time spent on many types of domestic labour may be decreasing, possibly due to the rise of such things as convenience food and cleaning, gardening and maintenance services for the home, it is interesting to note that some green tasks require more time and additional labour and which do not lend themselves to technological solutions. Recycling, for example, takes more time than unsorted waste disposal, and it is women who are more likely to undertake this extra labour (Oates and McDonald 2006). It is therefore not surprising that time is an important resource for the consumption work of domestic greening. Organo *et al.* (2013) report green householders placing importance on 'thinking time', to figure out how to implement more environmentally friendly practices, as well as the time required for more routine practices to take place. In Organo's study, such time was available to mainly wealthier households, where women had the option of working part-time, and were able to devote time to green tasks such as growing vegetables and looking after chickens that might otherwise have been spent in the workforce (lower income families) or looking after children (single parent households). Thus, when the labour-intensive nature of green activities is also time-consuming, those with less leisure time, or less time away from other responsibilities, will be less likely to spend that time on greening. Furthermore, for such 'middle-class households … homeowning families that are able to make the choice for the mothers to work part time, and who have control over structural decisions made about their house and garden, sustainability actions embody a certain sort of household identity .... as 'good' household managers' (Organo *et al.* 2013, 571).

> Meanwhile, men retained the idea of work and leisure time as temporally and spatially discrete. For them, sustainability was commonly understood as a leisure practice, a downtime after work. While men were often responsible for the labour and upfront time required to start, or research, a [green] household project, commonly the responsibility fell to women on an everyday basis to change habits, maintain or run a household project. Women, therefore, over time became more inclined to carry the load of sustainable practices.
>
> (Organo *et al.* 2013, 572)

Against these uneven temporal and social realities of domestic environmental labour, it is useful to posit an imaginary idealized 'domestic green labourer' in the green capitalist/ecological modernist logic, where natural resources are judged in terms of their 'productivity'. For example, in Australia, rainwater falling on concrete is often perceived as a wasted resource and pricing of mains water by usage (rather than access) is increasingly perceived as appropriate (Farbotko *et al.* 2014). Government is transferring some resource supply responsibilities to households (e.g. through mandating water tanks in new dwellings). There is also increasing complexity, especially in the context of privatization of utilities, with a range of governmental, quasi-governmental, private and civil society actors involved in activities such as water and electricity distribution, which were once typically state-based or community-based. Overall, it seems three roles are simultaneously ascribed to householders according to the ecological modernization logic in a capitalist global market:

1 Householders have a moral responsibility to conserve resources for the sake of the environment.
2 Householders are bearers of consumer rights to unlimited (or limited only by financial capacity) consumption.
3 Private property rights, which underscore the ideal of the private, liberal home, include the right to produce water, power, food and other resources for private use.

According to such populist ecological modernization logic, the ideal green citizen-consumer believes that conservation of resources is desirable and is willing to do so. However, this citizen-consumer also harbours a desire to continue to enjoy the same lifestyle that is imagined in business-as-usual capitalism (that is, outside the green economy.) Ecological modernization can, in theory, deliver both these dreams through increased consumption and technological innovations in the green market. Within this conceptualization, there are no neat boundaries around 'producers' and 'consumers': householders can be both when engaging in domestic greening (Gibson *et al.* 2011). Moreover, there are no neat boundaries between 'labour' and 'capital'. In the domestic setting, the householder can simultaneously be labourer and capitalist. However, the more capital is accumulated, the more likely certain labours will be outsourced (e.g. car-washing, gardening, cleaning, laundering clothes, cooking).

In practice, consumption of 'green technologies' involves significant work by the consumer (research, installation, maintenance, etc.) and technological innovation is never perfect, either in production or when put to use: technologies fail or break down in certain contexts, and information is incomplete or complex. The crucial point, however, is not that technologies fail or information is incomplete in and of itself. Rather, much domestic greening involves householders engaging *primarily* in 'green consumption work' aimed not only at purchasing green products, but also addressing technology and information failure. This consumption work does not necessarily materially and directly advance resource conservation. This is not to say that resource conservation is not a goal, and sometimes an outcome. However, to the extent that the myth of easy greening is accepted and the actual work of conservation is outsourced to various technologies, consumers are possibly absolving themselves of responsibility to do this work (Marres 2008).

Technologies typically cannot 'conserve' resources, they can only collect, store and distribute them. Products such as green detergents, water-efficient shower heads, and reusable cloth shopping bags are largely dependent on particular types of use: it is *people* who need to do the work to ensure not too much detergent is used in each wash; that the shopping bag is taken to the shop and used until it is completely worn out; that reduced water pressure in water-saving shower heads is not simply swapped for longer showers. Water tanks and solar panels are not typically equipped with sophisticated data collection and analysis mechanisms to ensure overall household consumption in relation to the grid is reduced over time. This is an important myth accompanying technological 'solutions': that green technologies somehow do the work of reducing consumption.

The myth of technology doing the work of reducing consumption is a powerful one, supported by the liberal ideal of a private home where the householder can create processes of inclusion and exclusion of Nature however they see fit:

> Socially conscious consumers pay attention to the collective good by meeting their individual private interests ... A socially conscious consumption lifestyle ... enlarges his or her own benefits and increases the return on his or her investment. [These consumers] garner a number

of rewards, mostly experiential, by positioning their self-interest as part of the consumption equation. These rewards and consumption choices also lead to a number of obstacles or burdens—information overload, logistical difficulties, restricted choice—that consumers have to resolve. This is done by reframing the costs as sources of enjoyment.

(Atkinson 2012, 202)

This quote, from a study of 'socially responsible consumption' suggests an expectation that the consumer do the work of translating difficulties and complexities of 'socially responsible consumption' into enjoyment. Furthermore, the beneficiary of this work in an ecologically modern imaginary is always the consumer's private interest as well as the public good. A problematic corollary of this pairing of private and public interest is that the public good typically only gets factored into decisions which also have a private benefit: in ecologically modernist theory and practice, Nature or 'the environment' is not often valued for its own sake at the domestic scale. When private property rights to collect resources are exercised, such production does not necessarily result in any net increase to the public good, as I will explore in the next chapter. Technology *per se*, in an ecologically modern home, does not ensure that the uses to which resources collected at home actually increase overall public good. Even among those consumers with strong green commitments, the temptation to use privately collected resources to increase rather than decrease household consumption might be strong:

> For socially conscious consumers … enacting citizenship through consumption reaps rewards for the individual while at the same time working toward meaningful social change at the local and global levels. [All] consumption choices entail a degree of effort and sacrifice, but these sacrifices are made willingly. Rather than focus on the cost (literal and figurative) of leading a socially conscious consumption lifestyle, informants focus on the enjoyment such compromises brought. By reframing the extra effort as a source of potential pleasure and as another possible benefit, the informants are able to reconcile the burdensome side of prosocial consumption with the self-interested, private motivations that underpin it.
>
> (Atkinson 2012, 201)

Atkinson's work is informed by Soper's (2007, 2008) model of 'alternative hedonism'. Alternative hedonism is a lifestyle philosophy that 'affirms the value of a good life that is not lived at the expense of social and environmental justice' (Vannini and Taggert 2016, 83; Soper 2007; 2008). As a 'a starting point to understand the synthesis of self and other in socially conscious consumption' this is not about pure selflessness or altruism in consumer choices. Rather, according to Atkinson, socially conscious consumers adopt a self-interested disaffection with consumerist consumption. The way such private interests play out in domestic greening consumption is of interest in the next chapter.

Summary

To conclude, this chapter has tried to show that a significant yet neglected phenomenon worthy of attention, is the upsurge in voluntary and yet mostly unrecognized domestic labour being undertaken for 'the environment'. There is a need to unpack, from different angles, the fact that the activities undertaken by householders in the name of the environment involve work (Cox 2013). While the ecological modernist desire to shift a significant portion of the burden of environmental responsibility onto consumers has been critiqued, the details of how this burden becomes translated into new forms of resource politics and social stratification through new divisions of emotional, physical and mental effort at the domestic scale is only beginning to be explored (Klocker *et al.* 2012; MacGregor 2011; Marres 2011; Mee *et al.* 2014; Organo *et al.* 2013). The next chapter takes up this task, discussing how different domestic greening labours can be understood in terms of the privatization of resources.

Notes

1 http://www.yourhome.gov.au/preface/welcome-your-home Last accessed 21 June 2016.
2 http://www.sanctuarymagazine.org.au/home/about-sanctuary-magazine/ Last accessed 21 June 2016.

References

Adams, M., & Raisborough, J. (2010). Making a difference: Ethical consumption and the everyday. *The British Journal of Sociology, 61*(2), 256–274.
Allon, F. (2008). *Renovation Nation: Our Obsession with Home.* Sydney: UNSW Press.
Atkinson, L. (2012). Buying in to social change: How private consumption choices engender concern for the collective. *The Annals of the American Academy of Political and Social Science, 644*(1), 191–206.
Barr, S., Shaw, G., & Coles, T. (2011). Times for (un) sustainability? Challenges and opportunities for developing behaviour change policy. A case-study of consumers at home and away. *Global Environmental Change, 21*(4), 1234–1244.

Bhatti, M. & Church, A. (2001). Cultivating natures: Homes and gardens in late modernity. *Sociology*, 35(2), 365–383.

Blunt, A. (2005). Cultural geography: Cultural geographies of home. *Progress in Human Geography*, 29(4), 505–515.

Brickell, K. (2012). Geopolitics of home. *Geography Compass*, 6(10), 575–588.

Cox, R. (2013). House/work: Home as a space of work and consumption. *Geography Compass*, 7(12), 821–831.

Craig, G. (2010). Everyday epiphanies: Environmental networks in eco-makeover lifestyle television. *Environmental Communication*, 4(2), 172–189.

Davison, A. (2011). A domestic twist on the eco-efficiency turn: Environmentalism, technology, home. In: A. Gorman-Murray and R. Lane (eds), *Material Geographies of Household Sustainability*. Surrey: Ashgate, 35.

Deutz, P. (2014). A class-based analysis of sustainable development: developing a radical perspective on environmental justice. *Sustainable Development*, 22(4), 243–252.

Farbotko, C., & Waitt, G. (2011). Residential air-conditioning and climate change: Voices of the vulnerable. *Health Promotion Journal of Australia: Official journal of Australian Association of Health Promotion Professionals*, 22(Special Issue), S13.

Farbotko, C., & Head, L. (2013). Gifts, sustainable consumption and giving up green anxieties at Christmas. *Geoforum*, 50, 88–96.

Farbotko, C., Walton, A., Mankad, A., & Gardner, J. (2014). Household rainwater tanks: Mediating changing relations with water?. *Ecology and Society*, 19(2).

Flichy, P. (2007). Understanding Technological Innovation: A Socio-Technical Approach. Cheltenham, UK: Edward Elgar Publishing.

Gibson, C., Head, L., Gill, N., & Waitt, G. (2011). Climate change and household dynamics: Beyond consumption, unbounding sustainability. *Transactions of the Institute of British Geographers*, 36(1), 3–8.

Gibson, C., Farbotko, C., Gill, N., Head, L., & Waitt, G. (2013). *Household Sustainability: Challenges and Dilemmas in Everyday Life*. Cheltenham, UK: Edward Elgar Publishing.

Gifford, R., & Nilsson, A. (2014). Personal and social factors that influence pro-environmental concern and behaviour: A review. *International Journal of Psychology*, 49(3), 141–157.

Gill, N., Osman, P., Head, L., Voyer, M., Harada, T., Waitt, G., & Gibson, C. (2015). Looking beyond installation: Why households struggle to make the most of solar hot water systems. *Energy Policy*, 87, 83–94.

Glucksmann, M. (2013). *Working to consume: Consumers as the missing link in the division of labour*. Centre for Research in Economic Sociology and Innovation (CRESI) Working Paper 2013-03, University of Essex: Colchester.

Gorman-Murray, A., McKinnon, S., & Dominey-Howes, D. (2014). Queer domicide: LGBT displacement and home loss in natural disaster impact, response, and recovery. *Home Cultures*, 11(2), 237–261.

Graham, S., & Thrift, N. (2007). Out of order: Understanding repair and maintenance. *Theory, Culture & Society*, 24(3), 1–25.

Head, L., & Gibson, C. (2012). Becoming differently modern: Geographic contributions to a generative climate politics. *Progress in Human Geography*, 36(6), 699–714.

Hinchliffe, S. (1996). Helping the earth begins at home: The social construction of socio-environmental responsibilities. *Global Environmental Change*, 6(1), 53–62.

Hobson, K. (2002). Competing discourses of sustainable consumption: Does the 'rationalisation of lifestyles' make sense?. *Environmental Politics*, 11(2), 95–120.

hooks, b. (1990). *Yearning: Race, Gender, and Cultural Politics*. Boston: South End Press.

Houston, D., & Ruming, K. (2014). Suburban toxicity: A political ecology of asbestos in Australian cities. *Geographical Research*, 52(4), 400–410.

Kaika, M. (2004). Interrogating the geographies of the familiar: Domesticating nature and constructing the autonomy of the modern home. *International Journal of Urban and Regional Research*, 28(2), 265–286.

Klinenberg, E. (2015). Heat wave: A social autopsy of disaster in Chicago. Chicago: University of Chicago Press.

Klocker, N., Gibson, C. & Borger, E. (2012). Living together but apart: Material geographies of everyday sustainability in extended family households. *Environment and Planning - A*, 44(9), 2240.

Krall, J.R., & Peng, R.D. (2015). The Volkswagen scandal: Deception, driving and deaths. *Significance*, 12(6), 12–15.

MacGregor, S. (2011). *Beyond Mothering Earth: Ecological Citizenship and the Politics of Care*. Vancouver: UBC Press.

Marres, N. (2008). The making of climate publics: Eco-homes as material devices of publicity. *Distinktion: Scandinavian Journal of Social Theory*, 9(1), 27–45.

Marres, N. (2011). The costs of public involvement: Everyday devices of carbon accounting and the materialization of participation. *Economy and Society*, 40(4), 510–533.

Mee, K. J., Instone, L., Williams, M., Palmer, J., & Vaughan, N. (2014). Renting over troubled waters: An urban political ecology of rental housing. *Geographical Research*, 52(4), 365–376.

O'Connor, M. (1994). Is sustainable capitalism possible? In: M. O'Connor (ed), *Is Capitalism Sustainable?: Political Economy and the Politics of Ecology*. New York: Guilford Press, 152–175.

Oates, C. J., & McDonald, S. (2006). Recycling and the domestic division of labour: Is green pink or blue?. *Sociology*, 40(3), 417–433.

Organo, V., Head, L., & Waitt, G. (2013). Who does the work in sustainable households? A time and gender analysis in New South Wales, Australia. *Gender, Place & Culture*, 20(5), 559–577.

Parker, J. K. M. (2013). *Saving Neoliberalism: Rudd Labor's Response to the 2008 Global Economic Crisis* (Doctoral dissertation). University of Technology, Sydney. http://hdl.handle.net/10453/29229

Potter, E., & Oster, C. (2008). Communicating climate change: Public responsiveness and matters of concern. *Media International Australia*, 127(1), 116–126.

Reid, K., & Beilin, R. (2015). Making the landscape 'home': Narratives of bushfire and place in Australia. *Geoforum, 58*, 95–103.

Shove, E. (2003). *Comfort, Cleanliness and Convenience: The Social Organization of Normality* (Vol. 810). Oxford: Berg.

Slocum, R. (2004). Consumer citizens and the cities for climate protection campaign. *Environment and Planning A, 36*(5), 763–782.

Smerecnik, K. R., & Renegar, V.R. (2010). Capitalistic agency: The rhetoric of BP's Helios Power campaign. *Environmental Communication, 4*(2), 152–171.

Soper, K. (2007). Re-thinking the Good Life: The citizenship dimension of consumer disaffection with consumerism. *Journal of Consumer Culture, 7*(2), 205–229.

Soper, K. (2008). Alternative hedonism, cultural theory and the role of aesthetic revisioning. *Cultural Studies, 22*(5), 567–587.

Vannini, P., & Taggart, J. (2016). Onerous consumption: The alternative hedonism of off-grid domestic water use. *Journal of Consumer Culture, 16*(1), 80–100.

Wheeler, K., & Glucksmann, M. (2015). *Household Recycling and Consumption Work: Social and Moral Economies*. London: Palgrave Macmillan.

Warrington, M. (2001). 'I must get out': The geographies of domestic violence. *Transactions of the Institute of British Geographers, 26*(3), 365–382.

3   Privatizing greening and the work of green technology

Working to green the home

Policy promoting domestic greening often involves attempts to increase installation of 'green' technologies for the home. Such technologies include energy-efficient lightbulbs and water-efficient showerheads, water tanks, insulation, and solar panels. It is worth considering the politics of some of these technologies. Davison (2011: 46–47) for example, considers that 'Australia's tradition of domestic introversion in the emerging preoccupation with domestic eco-efficiency [is relevant to] the continued failure of environmental movements to realize their political ends through strategies that regard technology merely as apolitical means.' Green technologies are often assumed to be socio-politically neutral yet financially beneficial, and therefore to appeal – at least to some extent – across political divides. Green technologies for the home are imagined, in normative greening agendas, to offer a kind of passive domestic greening that is ostensibly achieved largely by the technology itself. The bulk of the work of domestic greening, in other words, is assumed to be largely performable by non-human things, with people acting as operators or managers. The role of householders, according to this imaginary, is chiefly to buy and install, and perhaps eventually arrange for servicing or replacing, of green products. This role is more about the accumulation of capital, green or otherwise, than the undertaking of green labour *per se* by humans.

As it turns out, domestic greening labour for humans and technologies is typically far from straightforward. Installation and use of green technology is often a complex undertaking involving new ideas, understandings, skills and products, that can have contradictory, and not necessarily environmentally sound, outcomes (Gill *et al.* 2015). The work that householders do to research, locate, organize, analyze, troubleshoot and maintain their domestic greening products is considerable and becoming recognized in some areas of research as a barrier to more domestic greening. For example:

Information that aims to encourage homeowners to install solar systems is plentiful, but households do the hard work of figuring it all out … consumers are encouraged to find out which system best suits their household size, location, house configuration, and climate, to work out the relative installation and running costs of different systems, to conduct research on these issues and to seek 'expert advice'.

(Gibson *et al*. 2013, 147)

In this chapter, I focus on some of the resource politics of green technologies and domestic environmental labour. These politics can vary, perhaps ultimately unsurprisingly, in some ways reproducing elements of wider, dominant systems of resource use beyond the household. As will be explored, a desire to privatize control of resources for domestic purposes is often coterminous with domestic greening activities. Privatization, in capitalist thinking, is moralized as being both democratic and paradisiacal, emanating 'the promise of a scarce-free palette of choices to satisfy all material and immaterial human needs' (Ahlers and Zwarteveen 2009, 413). Domestic greening often seems to be carried out with this promise in mind, albeit at a domestic scale. For many, the idea of sacrificing comfort is ultimately less appealing than the alternative, that environmental conservation is available without decreasing current standards of living. Indeed, as will be explored, the appeal of private comfort afforded by sometimes labour-intensive domestic products for collection and supply of power and water, unfettered by the prices of big business and the regulations of government (for example, water restrictions) is sometimes stronger than the desire to conserve resources. Domestic greening technologies, although intended mostly to do the work of 'saving resources', can quite easily be appropriated into a different political (and material) liberal project, namely, collecting and using resources such as rainwater *as the householder sees fit*, without quantitative reductions in consumption levels. The fact that much policy and research on domestic greening sees two ultimately separate projects – domestic greening and private domestic control of resources – as having commensurable values and outcomes is an indication of how far ecological modernization thinking is entrenched as common sense.

As has been examined in the previous chapter, domestic environmental activity, in a broad sense, is rarely studied as a form of labour, and yet domestic labour is fundamental to the green political economy. Typically, actions directed towards environmental care, at home or anywhere else, are conceived in research and policy in terms of behaviours or as social practices, and sometimes as a form of consumerist citizenship. A practices-approach might focus, for instance, on the conveniences normalized through habit in domestic life, such as the convenience of using a garden sprinkler or hose, compared to the inconvenience of carrying water in buckets or watering cans to the garden (Mee *et al.* 2014). Thus the act of carrying water using human labour is conceived as a barrier to achieving a social norm (convenience). Carrying water involves more labour than does turning on a tap and directing a garden hose. However, the labour involved is not only an inconvenience. Carrying water involves physical exertion, and this has bodily effects, as well as (perhaps) environmental and/or economic effects, as well as social outcomes. Bodily effects of domestic environmental labour can be unrelated to the environment, and be both negative (*it's tiring and my arms get sore*) and positive (*it keeps me fit*); labour is undertaken and this labour has multiple effects. The hose, to take this example further, is a technology intended to replace the need for human labour for transporting water to achieve a particular domestic task, such as watering the garden. For a committed, hypothetical domestic greener, however, a hose might be viewed less positively, as a way of facilitating water wastage. For such a domestic greener, reintroduction of buckets collecting shower water, replacing a hose *for the sake of the environment* seems to minimize use of a water wasting technology. It also reintroduces extra labour, in the form of transporting buckets of water using human muscles. This human labour might be an inconvenience for the hypothetical domestic greener, or perhaps more positively described as a labour of love for the environment, or both. Regardless, a domestic greener might be *more* willing to carry heavy buckets of captured shower water around the domestic space than to relinquish particular private goods, such as regular showers or a well-watered garden. Thus, human labour, in this example, might function to reduce volumes of water used in the domestic space, but there is no assurance of such an outcome. In the absence of reduced showers taken, only excess or waste water is rechanneled through human labour. There is no challenge to other, private uses of the resource. Such work, moreover, is increasingly being 'delegated' by domestic greeners to technologies, such as water tanks.

Installing a water tank for the purpose of watering the garden does seem more sensible than carrying water in buckets collected in the shower to the garden. However, it is sensible not because water tanks are somehow better at 'saving' water than buckets; it is because a tank used instead of shower water carried in buckets to the garden saves human *labour.* A water tank, moreover, is not inherently better at collecting water than a bucket. A water tank *can* sometimes do the work of collecting water better than buckets – when it is big and there is more rain falling in its catchment than is captured in buckets in the shower. This depends, in turn, on how long the householders shower for, the capacity of the shower head, how many showerers there are, how many showers are taken per person per day, and the number and size of the buckets used to capture shower water. Thus a water tank can collect water well. However, when there is no rain, the buckets in the shower will be better at collecting water, assuming the house is connected to mains water for personal water use (the norm in Australia) and householders continue to take some showers. The garden can still get watered, but someone will need to carry heavy buckets of water to the garden. Either way, neither the tank nor the bucket does any work to *conserve* water, only to collect it. The importance is in perception of waste: rainwater falling on roofs or mains water falling on shower floors and running back into stormwater drains is perceived as 'wasted', and attempts to reduce this waste are seen as beneficial. Indeed, ecological modernization often focusses on addressing such inefficiencies rather than addressing excess consumption *per se.* Thus, when water is collected in a tank installed in the garden, or in buckets in the shower, it is perceived as 'saved', and this is often glossed as inherently green. Water conservation, however, does not necessarily occur when excess water is 'saved'. Overall, water is conserved when it is used in less volume than before, not when the overall consumption *status quo* is maintained or possibly increased. For example, when the garden is watered from a newly installed tank, overall supply and hence consumption can increase. Water tanks, perhaps more so than buckets which are very heavy, very convincingly *appear* to do the labour of conserving resources for us. They are perceived to perform the task of 'saving' water simply by existing, and this easily translates into a belief that water has been conserved.

In this context, it is not trite to observe that any domestic technology, green or otherwise, such as hot water systems, toilets and refrigerators are things that get noticed more when they *fail* than when they *work* (Gibson *et al.* 2013). While any failure of domestic technology to perform its primary function (providing hot water, flushing sanitary waste away, keeping food cold) is likely to be of utmost concern, such breakdown is often easily and immediately observable to the sensory receptors of the non-expert – the typical householder. Less likely to be discernable to a non-expert is a failure of a particular technology to perform a perceived green function, a reduction in quantity of the resource used. It is not immediately obvious, for example, whether or not a water tank is reducing domestic water consumption. To confirm reductions in water consumption, it would likely be necessary to do a longitudinal analysis of water bills (where mains water is still available, as is usual) and compare this analysis with measurements of rainwater collection and usage sourced from the tank. Such data is not necessarily readily available and would require some householder ingenuity and commitment.

Just as Shove (2003) demonstrated that the washing machine is not used to 'consume water and power' but to achieve social standards of cleanliness and convenience, similarly, engaging in domestic greening can be undertaken to conform with current social standards of resource use. Such standards may purport to be green. For example, many flourishing public gardens in Australia, where drought is common, now bear signage 'tank water in use'. This is a telling declaration of a particular resource politics: it corresponds to contemporary public perceptions in Australia that mains water is becoming too valuable to use for watering public decorative gardens. It is also a statement about a perceived lesser value of tank water relative to mains water. Very rarely are the remains of a dying or dead garden to be seen with a sign declaring 'any type of water too precious to maintain drought-intolerant plants'. While the cultural and public health values of public gardens are also significant in this resource politics, it is important to note that the work of installing water tanks for the purpose of nurturing decorative gardens is not just technical and physical, it is also social and political. In a similar fashion, it is worth considering that very often, green products are bought and used ostensibly to *reduce* consumption but also to gain other types of green capital such as supporting the embryonic green market or claiming a green social status. Meanwhile, some domestic environmental labour offers no direct benefit for household members, apart from the altruistic benefit of doing something good for the environment. There are no clean clothes or meals prepared when the recycling is sorted from other types of waste; and maintaining solar hot water systems may actually provide less opportunity for a reliably warm shower than conventional hot water systems (Gill *et al.* 2015; Oates and McDonald 2006). What is less obvious is that green capital, in other cases, can be flexible and readily available to householders and others to further a range of interests, some non-green, some private, some economic. Various examples are explored in the remainder of this chapter.

Standalone houses versus apartments

It is interesting to consider some of the uneven distributions of domestic greening initiatives. In high-income nations such as Australia, 'low-income households and women are already doing much of the work of sustainability without grandstanding it' (Gibson *et al.* 2013, 184). On the other hand, 'it is relatively affluent populations and households, often with a high interest in, and commitment to, sustainability, who continue to live unsustainably by virtue of their ability to consume' (Waitt *et al.* 2012, 68). Some might contend that if high-consuming households spend more on domestic greening initiatives, then this expenditure is an adequate trade-off for the high consumption of these households. The danger here is assuming that high levels of consumption can be equitably negated by domestic greening technologies. A six-bedroom, two-car garage home for a family of four with a grey-water system, a water tank and solar panels does not necessarily have a lower environmental or social impact than a three-bedroom apartment, near public transport which is used frequently, with no retrofitted green technologies. Nevertheless, high-consuming households are often considered important in domestic greening when they function as green trend-setters. While early uptake of highly visible, sophisticated technologies, including whole homes designed by green architects may be helpful to an extent, many households simply cannot afford such expenses (Moy 2012; Gill *et al.* 2015). Lower income households can be green simply by having less money to spend on flights, large cars, air-conditioning and so on. Lower income domestic greening activities are likely to involve lower green capital such as reusing family bath water or synchronizing toilet usage with other family members to minimize water used for flushing (Farbotko and Head 2013; Gibson *et al.* 2013).

In Australia, it is households with relatively high incomes and who are title holders (mortgagees or home owners) rather than tenants, who have greater capacity to engage in the dominant, most socially visible versions of domestic greening – that is, consumption of (often expensive) green products and purchasing of eco-efficient technologies (Altmann 2014). Purchasers of green products ostensibly contribute to both economic growth and reduced environmental impact (Waitt *et al.* 2012), while the 'building's physical changes that accompany environmentally sustainable retrofits become statements about the values of the owners and occupants' (Altmann 2014, 440). 'The home' in domestic greening policies in Australia is often imagined as an individual standalone dwelling with outside space. The free-standing home on a quarter-acre block has long stood as the embodiment of the Great Australian Dream, although higher density dwellings (including high end apartments) that include communally managed common spaces are increasing in number (Allon 2008; Altmann 2014). The policy focus on free-standing dwellings has implications for the distribution of domestic greening activities. In Australia 'retrofitting initiatives for existing housing stock largely ignore the growth in apartment dwellings and strata title developments, since they are given to individual owners rather than owner corporations' (Altmann 2014, 438). Altmann (2014, 440) notes 'this may be due to the high levels of home ownership in Australia and the fact that much of the population's wealth is in home ownership.' Thus it is not just the size and type of dwelling that is differentiated in mainstream ideas about domestic greening, but also the type of tenure, which is often, although certainly not always, correlated with wealth in the Australian context. However, it is generally the case in Australia that public and private housing tenants are afforded fewer opportunities to participate in government programs for domestic greening (Altmann 2014; Farbotko and Waitt 2011):

Tenants in the residential rental housing market in Australia are vulnerable in a world of changing climate due to the legislation that governs and restricts what changes they can make to the physical fabric of their homes, their lack of access to green rebate schemes, and often their reduced financial capacity.

(Mee *et al.* 2014, 366)

I just want it to be easy to be sustainable.

(Tenant cited in Mee *et al.* 2014, 374)

Mee *et al.* (2014) describe tenants in Australia needing to obtain landlord permission for vegetable gardens, water-saving installations, and energy-efficiency measures: these are extra hurdles for tenants interested in greening their rental properties.

It is not necessarily the same elsewhere. In Sweden, for example, building managers have made recycling easier for apartment dwellers, rather than single-dwelling households (Wheeler 2013). However, if water tanks and solar panels are typical expressions of the ecological modernist green household in Australia, then those with greatest access to green cultural capital seem to be those who own and live in detached housing and have enough liquid finance to bear the significant expense of their purchase and installation (Altmann 2014). The motivation for such greening in Australia is a complex mixture of environmental care, increasing market value of the property, a performance of a particular social identity, and in some cases, state-level government mandates.

Ecological modernist domestic greening is thus more accessible to freehold land title holders in Australia than to the increasing population of high-density dwellings, with common space and common management proving to be a significant barrier to achieving greening in such dwellings (Altman 2014). Altmann (2014) points out that it takes a dedicated group of tenants working together with one vision to enact the substantial and often costly measures to green an apartment building in Australia. Altmann (2014) notes a push by the green private sector to work with owner-corporations in high-density apartment developments; green suppliers are beginning to see value in high-density apartments as an untapped market, which to date have been neglected by government incentives aimed at individual dwellings. Further, green technologies are seen by such actors as making good business sense regardless of whether or not those involved were interested in environmental outcomes. However, procedural and policy barriers exist to dampen what might otherwise be an efficient green market. In Altmann's study, not only did 'greening committee' members need to source the appropriate information and cost of the various domestic greening technologies, they had to undertake considerable negotiation with the existing owner group, government and statutory bodies, and their strata managers in order to determine possible outcomes. The difficulty of negotiating collective decision-making was noted by one owner as an impediment to the implementation of energy-efficient measures in her apartment:

> If I lived in an independent home, I would probably have taken up [energy and water efficiency] options that I just choose not to take up because I can't be bothered negotiating them. So, you know there are kind of planetary consequences from the fact that I am part of this organisation.
>
> (Altmann 2014, 447)

Off-gridding

While tenants and lower-income households in Australia face policy obstacles to some domestic greening, the 'off-grid' movement involves householders, usually with freehold title over the land, attempting to decouple from centralized infrastructure and to be self-sufficient in resources such as water and power. Vannini and Taggart (2014, 64) have described off-gridding in terms of a 'thorough reinvention and reassembling of the technologies and resources needed to generate and experience everyday bodily comforts'. According to Vannini and Taggart, off-grid living is 'the living condition of a household or a community lying outside the electricity infrastructure, but often also denotes disconnection from other infrastructures such as municipal water conduits, natural gas pipelines, road networks, garbage and waste collection, food supply chains, and telecommunications' (Vannini and Taggart 2013, 295). The politics of such disconnection can vary, of course, by individual household, but Vannini and Taggart see domestic greening as central to the off-gridding project. Domestic greening is considered to be achievable to off-gridders because resource flows are more apparent, and householders are more actively engaged in resource collection and harnessing:

> Off-gridders reverse the typical orientation toward the Western bourgeois home as separate from and independent of an untamed "nature" found outside its walls ... by taking an active role in collecting, storing, utilizing, and disposing of natural resources and by becoming physically involved in how water is channelled in and out of their homes. By doing so, off-gridders turn potentially unreflexive, habitual, and mindless routine domestic activities into going concerns. Off-grid living, in other words, consists of making inconspicuous everyday

domestic practices conspicuous and meaningful, and thus the nexus of conservation.

(Vannini and Taggart 2013, 95–96)

There is an expectation that resource–limits will be more readily apparent to domestic users when produced at the domestic scale (such as water tanks running dry or generators failing), leading to less wastage and less overall consumption. For off-gridders, the modern home is not conceived primarily as a site of leisure, although 'everyday bodily comforts', as quoted above, are typically valued. Leisure is not dismissed, but off-gridding does reject some of the 'easy greening' aspects of ecological modernization. Off-gridding is a more radical and more overtly political type of domestic greening; far from being a dominant or mainstream activity, it is unusual in that it often recognizes domestic greening as labour-intensive. Indeed, the value and practise of hard work have been posited as central to the project of off-gridding (Vannini and Taggart 2013). For example:

> Offgridders' entanglements with water constitute a type of onus—a burden, but an enjoyable one, and a treasured responsibility of (relative) self-sufficiency. We refer to their engagement with water as onerous consumption—a type of consumption characterized by wilfully chosen burdensome involvement. Though it is the source of some degree of inconvenience, toil, and occasionally technical problems, this onus is uniformly appreciated by all off-gridders, and is indeed recognized to be a self-fulfilling moral responsibility and even a treasured privilege of their chosen lifestyle.
>
> (Vannini and Taggart 2013, 4)

Off-gridding is, for some, a type of ethical consumption that celebrates purposeful human labour as a way of rejecting consumerism:

> Onerous consumption refers therefore to a type of consumption characterized by a problematizing stance toward the act of consuming—a moral stance that recognizes the broader socio-environmental consequences of consumption and that manifests itself through practices of alternative engagement with place, natural resources, and the material world. Onerous consumption is a counter-hegemonic, self-reflective, and critical orientation that rejects the seductive appeal of an unrestrained consumerism that promises a carefree, inconvenience-free, endless gratification of "needs" and desires. The burdens of onerous consumption are, however, not overwhelmingly painful or unbearably disagreeable responsibilities that one should like to escape. Rather,

they are moral and practical obligations and orientations woven into ordinary routines and accepted and even embraced as inevitable necessities of one's everyday existence. Onerous consumption depends on the consumer's direct, embodied, and permanent involvement in the process of collecting, storing, channelling, and disposing of the subject matter of consumption.

(Vannini and Taggart 2013, 5)

Off-gridders do, at times, find their work taxing:

The extra mundane work an off-grid cabin requires—the wood-chopping, the heating, collecting water, the difficulties with cooking and storing food, and all that jazz—inevitably means that at least one of [a couple] be employed no more than part-time. While they find time to read to each other and do creative work, they long for a somewhat easier life, perhaps in a cob or straw bale house somewhere warmer, at least in the not so distant future.

(Vannini and Taggart 2013, 299)

For off-gridders, there remains appeal in domestic leisure, apparently at least partially achievable by moving house and changing climate.

Off-gridders sometimes seem to be wary; trusting neither governments nor dominant markets to properly care for the environment or for citizens. For this reason, resource needs are perceived as needing to be satisfied at a smaller scale, sometimes within a community but often within a household. For these off-gridders, domestic greening is not necessarily the primary aim. When not centrally motivated by environmental considerations, social and economic goals seem more important to some off-gridders – perhaps more so – than environmental ones. On Yourway.org.au, for example, which promises 'Affordable Comfortable Abundance – how to live off the grid', the site's creators' pursue freedom from dominant systems of provision, with sustainability a beneficial, but minor, side-effect:

Chances are you're tired of struggling to make money, and want to be free to live your way. You know it is possible but don't yet know how. You are searching for affordable and practical solutions. This site will teach you everything you need …. Think of the time and effort you put into making money. What if you put this energy into creating a sustainable life? If you think this involves camping or chasing rabbits for dinner, you'd be wrong. It [sic] simply about using existing and affordable technology to reduce your expenses. You would live a normal life and just wouldn't "rely" on money. You could still have a job if you choose and in fact most people do, but the main difference is living would be cheaper so you work less. Your main expenses would be the occasional groceries, and any luxuries or recreational expenses. You will keep much more of the money you earn and have freedom to live your way.

In this particular version of off-gridding, there is a central role for technology, some sort of 'normal' life is deemed desirable, and leisure is important. Other statements on Yourway.org.au, contesting Vannini and Taggart's conclusions about onerous consumption, downplay the need for human labour in off-grid living. On Yourway.org.au there is also a transferral of labour towards purposes deemed more valuable than 'running the rat race'. The manifesto unfolds as follows on Yourway.org.au:

- *'Food grows from the ground, and water falls from the sky. You require only basic tools, and only a few minutes of work each day for an abundant supply'*. Here, labour required for self-sufficiency seems to be minimal.
- *'Think of the time and effort you put into making money. What if you put this energy into creating a sustainable life?'* Labour for 'sustainable life' is deemed more valuable than labour for cash.
- *'Usually most of the energy is consumed from appliances like TVs and refrigerators, which are easily run from affordable solar electricity equipment without grid connection.'* Technological solutions for domestic energy production are, apparently, simple and cheap.
- *'You don't "need" to grow your own food, but with the right technology its very easy.'* Technological solutions seem to be available for much domestic food production, minimizing the human labour required for growing food.
- *'Correct management of human waste is virtually automated once appropriate technology is installed.'* Technological solutions for domestic human waste management mirror "flush and forget" mentality that is highly valued in centralized systems.
- *'This opportunity is for people that are not afraid to take control of their own life. Real people are already doing it. You do not need to share resources if you don't want to. You can have all the privacy you want. This is about living life your way.'* This version of off-gridding values individual freedom and control more than communal resource use or public/social good.
- *'Is living getting easier, or more difficult? Take control of your own life.'* Off-gridding seems to allows greater opportunity for the exercise of individual freeom than the dominant political economy.

- '*We have the technology that enables us to live a free life in complete comfort – the way life should be.*' Comfort and freedom are revered; technology enables these.
- '*Nothing can set you free better than being able to live off your own land so you never even need money. But the laws make this very difficult.*' Freedom seems to be gained from private property ownership and use that is unfettered by government regulation.
- '*Most end up in the hands of bankers because of how the global financial system works. It is not their fault. It is your fault for supporting their system.*' Individuals have responsibility for delivering themselves from systemic inequities; the systemic inequities themselves are not addressed.

Important to many off-gridders is the 'sense of self-reliance and self-efficacy, independence' which makes whatever labour is undertaken worthwhile, sometimes expressed in terms of retreating and decoupling from both capitalism and the state. However, the retreat of many off-gridders is typically partial. Decoupling from communication (e.g. internet) and institutional (e.g. cash) systems, for example, is sometimes attempted but not as visible as decoupling from water and power grids in off-gridding manifestos and studies of off-grid life. Further, some types of resource decoupling seem to be more valued than others. Domestic water collection and power generation are mentioned more frequently than say, domestic clothing production – a typically feminized activity – suggesting that a gendered politics is significant.

Arguably worth considering is whether the pleasures and hardships of self-reliance and independence in off-grid life are the privilege of those with access to private property, either individually or communally. Would such access need to have been acquired while still 'on-grid'? Further, does material decoupling from the grid also involve decoupling from liberal, Enlightenment values such as privacy, and individual freedom? Such questions are relevant but rarely discussed, for instance, as a legacy of ungreen capitalism or colonialism. Those living off-grid may see their self-sufficiency in terms of a clean slate, but is their retreat into off-grid living made possible by historical involvement in particular political and economic relations? For example, Vannini and Taggart's somewhat unrealistic (and possibly classist) classification of off-gridders with 'modest' means includes those who inherited an island from their grandparents and with access to Can$50,000 on which to build a house on it. Another couple had Can$60,000 available to spend on installing off-grid systems sufficient to power 'all the typical appliances and conveniences of a suburban home' at least part of the time, including a hot-tub on the porch. Social stratification in on-grid living can be relevant to the choice to live off-grid. Vannini and Taggart (2013, 309) optimistically describe 'the off-grid lifeworld not as a utopian space of political transformation but rather as a quietist, heterotopic'. Pickerill (2015), more outwardly focussed, argues that 'pockets of alternative ways of being often connect and have influence far beyond their apparent remit, however small-scale or marginal they might appear. It can be in the off-grid alternative spaces of eco-communities that these alternatives get tested'. However, from another perspective, there is an 'othering' politics at work in off-gridding. Defining its resource politics in relation to infrastructure, some members of the off-grid movement seem uninclined to learn from those in the Global South, where entire communities have never even had the privilege of connection to a grid in the first place.

Suburban water tanks

Labour associated with domestic greening is, typically, part of broader networks of resource use. Homes that are disconnected from centralized systems of production of clean water, power, and food are rare in the Global North. Much more typically, there are deep interconnections – financial, material, social and political – between private homes and external systems, and these are in flux. Domestic sites in Australia, for instance, were once conceived simply as end-of-pipe destinations for centralized, state-owned water infrastructure. In a context of increasing deregulation and privatization of public infrastructure and a changing climate, however, free-standing suburban homes in particular are being re-imagined as appropriate sites for some water collection and storage through the use of domestic rainwater tank technology (Farbotko *et al.* 2014). Suburban domestic water tank use has attained popular and political appeal in Australia: the model of state provision of (unlimited) drinking-quality water for all domestic uses with price based on access, is changing to one of deregulation, pricing based on usage, and diversification of supply. In times of drought in Australia, there have been politically risky situations where government has been unable to guarantee mains water. The imposition of water restrictions during drought is unpopular. Although largely observed, water restrictions are often followed by policy promises to diversify supply – financed through increasing water prices - to avoid the need for future water restrictions. Thus, a message of unrestricted water consumption is enshrined in policy, tempered perhaps by an additional policy imperative to advance education about water as an increasingly scarce resource, and the promotion of voluntary water efficiency measures.

In this context, the domestic water tank is widely believed to 'save' otherwise wasted rainwater falling on suburban landscapes (Farbotko *et al.* 2014).

In Australian suburbs, tank water is not typically channeled for drinking or washing – this water remains largely sourced from the mains for health reasons. Tank water, however, is useful to householders for purposes other than drinking, cooking and showering (Moy 2012). The use to which such water is put is often to replace increasingly expensive mains water with unpriced tank water for gardening and other outdoor purposes. Tank water is also used to 'reclaim' water denied under mains water restrictions during times of drought. It is possible to wash the car, for example, using tank water but not mains water during water restrictions. Such uses of tank water have resulted in less than expected overall reductions in household mains water use when tanks are installed (Moy 2012). Rainwater, for some households, is thus seen as a scarce good over which private considerations can dominate (Farbotko *et al.* 2014). Water-tank owners in Australia have even expressed a preference to operate their tanks according to central tenets of neoliberalism, including that regulation of water consumption activities by the state should be minimal, and any water collected in tanks should be available only for private, discretionary use (Farbotko *et al.* 2014).

Households do not necessarily see their water tanks as being of direct financial benefit. In Farbotko *et al.* (2014), tank owners specified that their tanks did not contribute significantly to reduced household water bills, particularly after tank outlay and operating costs of attached electric pumps were taken into account. Householders saw value in tank water's ability to provide a way around water restrictions and other types of government intervention into water use. Households indicated a greater desire for control over water collected in their tanks than for financial benefit. Such tank owners certainly tend to express a public duty to conserve water supplies for the collective good, but more in terms of a narrative of tanks as somehow inherently 'water saving' devices. If only lip service is paid to the goal of conservation of public water supply, and there are no significant net decreases in household water consumption, closer attention to tank use should be paid (Moy 2012; Farbotko *et al.* 2014). If suburban water tank owners typically perceive of tanks as 'water saving' devices, and yet the domestic activities associated with tank water reveal a more complicated politics, perhaps this 'water saving' narrative needs to be questioned. In common sense understandings, water tanks are unquestionably environmental heroes, their installation seeming somehow to guarantee that green work is being done. Yet it is not terribly accurate to label tanks as water saving devices. Rather, they increase supply.

Undeniably, many domestic greeners are willing and able to work very hard at certain tasks, such as carrying water in buckets. Tank owners do engage in the labour of arranging installation and maintenance, and monitoring and drawing on the tank for various household uses. An insidious form of conceptual laziness however, allows slippage between 'collecting water', 'saving water' and 'reducing overall water usage' as if they are one and the same thing. The differences are neither subtle nor unimportant. Within the conceptual slippage, there is arguably a sanctioning of the continued exercise of consumer rights to consumption and the furthering of private interests.

Recycling

Turning now to consider how some domestic environmental labour is implicated in economic markets extending well beyond the household. Household recycling – or separating certain waste materials from others before collection by local authority waste services – is an activity that was, only half a generation ago, unheard of, but is now commonplace. Putting out the recycling is more than mundane household practice and it is more than an expression of environmental care (Oates and McDonald 2006). It is an additional task, for the environmentally minded, that has been added to the existing demands of domestic work:

> Recycling is shown to be related to the routine behaviours of housework and, therefore, often organised unequally between household members, particularly men and women ... Recycling is also located within relationships between people and is a source of 'warm feelings' that result from doing the right thing ... this labour is embedded in relationships and hierarchies of power.
>
> (Cox 2013, 828)

Recycling processes rely on householders regularly performing a range of waste cleaning, sorting and delivering tasks. Although these tasks may not always be categorized by them as 'work', recycling activities conducted in the domestic setting nevertheless are interdependent with external markets. Markets are not isolated from the context in which they are intended to function, being shaped by formal laws, social interaction and historic relations of production. Some markets function well, for instance, because unequal relations within the household provide unpaid domestic labour, buttressing the paid economy (Ahlers and Zwarteveen 2009). The labour undertaken by householders in household recycling (for which in Australia there is, on the whole, no form of payment) supports the recycling industry:

> As an industry recycling can function only with the assistance of free labor from households, this underpins its economic viability. But the people who perform this labor do not experience themselves

as volunteer workers in the recycling industry. They do not generally assess their actions as economically relevant. Rather, in performing the actions of a "recycler" they think of themselves as doing something good for nature and the environment. They see themselves as performing ethical, not economic, work.

(Hawkins 2006, 107)

Hawkins (2006) analyzed a government report on recycling, finding that:

Householders, through their time and effort, currently bear the primary cost of waste separation and sorting. This activity is fundamental to the operations of the recycling industry; without it recycling would not be economically feasible. The report acknowledges that the economic benefits of recycling depend on specific household practices voluntarily and willingly carried out by the population; and that this voluntary contribution has taken place in the face of steadily increasing charges for domestic waste removal.

(Hawkins 2006, 107)

Hawkins goes on to note:

There has been no economic incentive for householders to embrace the new classification and separation activities that recycling demands. Most are paying more for restricted waste services that involve more personal effort. How, then, do householders calculate the benefits of recycling? … as entirely ethical; they recycled because they were 'motivated by a concern for the environment.'

If householders do not regard their domestic recycling activities as economic work, this may be in part because recycling has typically been introduced into the domestic setting as an environmental not an economic activity. When local authorities introduced household recycling, labelling the often time-consuming and drudge-like recycling activities as 'volunteer work for the waste industry' may have resulted in lower levels of involvement in the practise. A green ethic is the motivation for householders to provide voluntary labour for an emergent industry. Hawkins goes on to argue that it is:

Impossible to reduce this waste practice to a purely economic logic. Instead, what is revealed is a network of practices and benefits that are heterogeneous and not entirely coherent. As an industry recycling can function only with the assistance of free labor from households, this underpins its economic viability. But the people who perform this labor do not experience themselves as volunteer workers in the recycling industry. They do not generally assess their actions as economically relevant. Rather, in performing the actions of a "recycler" they think of themselves as doing something good for nature and the environment. They see themselves as performing ethical, not economic, work.

(Hawkins 2006, 107)

Householders sort their waste, 'initiating a new economic process, providing feedstock (such as metals, plastics and paper) which in turn creates jobs/profits within the recycling, processing and manufacturing industries' (Wheeler and Glucksmann 2015, 551). In short, a whole industry is built on the voluntary, ecologically driven work of householders:

Consumers act as suppliers, warehousers, and distributors of materials which are then appropriated by the producer organisation, FTI, and municipalities. The consumer plays an integral role in the division of labour within waste management and the materials and energy economy depends upon and presupposes the completion of this work by consumers for its reproduction.

(Wheeler 2013, 33)

Although this [domestic recycling] work has a non-market character, its performance underpins the global market for material re-use.

(Wheeler 2013, 26)

And yet this work is largely unrecognized – by householders themselves and the industries they support. Wheeler (2013) argues that the work consumers perform in preparing their waste for recycling should be recognized as a significant and integral component of the division of labour within waste management. In Wheeler's study of recycling in Sweden, she reported that consumers were on the whole largely happy to participate in rather onerous domestic recycling separation work, based on a sense of environmental citizenship as well as a perception that doing so reduced the fees paid for waste-management. In another study, also in Sweden, only one participant recognized that recycling was a potentially profit-making activity reliant on the unpaid labour of the householder/consumer. This participant stated:

It is all about making money on garbage. There are a lot of people who make enormous amounts of money off it, but it is the people who pay, people who give away voluntarily something that has value. … if I take my car to the recycling station, it costs me 40 Swedish crowns to take it there … it is a cost for the environment and then there is a company that makes money out of it.

(Skill 2008, 250)

Domestic recycling tasks somehow manage to be both boring and complex; it never seems to be clear what is recyclable, and what should go to land-fill. In Wheeler and Glucksmann's (2015) study a waste management expert joked that 'consumers need a PhD in material science to correctly recycle their household waste', but the industry seems to remain a viable concern even though much waste is sorted incorrectly. Household recycling can suffer from the fatigue associated with mundane tasks that do not directly return a benefit to the household: the interesting, challenging labour is out-side the home. Further, if householders continue to engage in reflection on their role as voluntary labourers in a private industry, a green ethic of care may no longer be enough to stimulate household recycling work.

Outsourcing domestic environmental labour

Domestic greening is always political and implicated in broader mar-kets. The case of the off-gridders demonstrated that the domestication of alternative technologies can be burdensome. Such technologies often also require significant skills. Since not everyone has the capacity or time to acquire such skills, outsourcing tasks such as installation of solar panels can shift consumption work back into the realm of paid, market-based work. Domestic environmental labour in this way can become paid and formalized (Glucksmann 2013). Yet, such work still needs to be considered as domes-tic environmental labour for certain purposes. In a tragic, extreme case of harmful green technology, four unskilled installers of home insulation were killed in a poorly designed and executed federal government incen-tive 'Home Insulation Program' to increase uptake in Australia (Dollery and Hovey 2010; Kortt and Dollery 2012). The same scheme resulted in 120 house fires. Following the global financial crisis of 2008-2009, the Australian federal government at the time introduced an economic stimulus package, part of which involved an attempt to boost the green economy by providing householders with free home insulation to reduce energy used for heating and cooling. The presumption was a win-win-win for small green businesses and low-skilled workers who were installing the insulation, for the householders who could access green technology for both environmen-tal and financial benefits, and for the government who was trying to find ways for the economy to recover from the global financial crisis.

In a rush by households and small businesses to take advantage of the scheme, many workers (often young, un-unionized apprentices) became unwittingly involved in what turned out to be extremely unsafe working conditions. Demand was great, and insulation was imported from overseas, some of which may not have performed its insulation functions properly and also did not meet Australian standards. Without adequate training, the installation of insulation proved to easily cause electrocution. The deaths and fires during the Home Insulation Program were the result of inexperienced and untrained workers, with existing regulations grossly insufficient to protect them. One of the assumptions of government in introducing the Home Insulation Program was that the existing insulation market would deliver the program with speed, while ensuring probity and safety. However, the Home Insulation Program was also 'built around the belief that the million householders receiving the insulation free of cost would be able to act as "informed buyers" and regulate the quality and safety of the insulation being installed in their ceilings ... In fact householders seemed largely oblivious to safety issues and quality concerns until these were highlighted in the media' (Parker 2013). In the rush to achieve economic stimulus, safety issues were not given sufficient consideration and indeed the safety risks were transferred to the small businesses and householders, both groups having insufficient knowledge of the issues involved:

> The design of the Home Insulation Program gave extremely limited powers of regulation to [government, who] celebrated this 'light touch' regulation because it allowed the market greater scope to flourish and rapidly implement the Home Insulation Program.
>
> (Parker 2013, 235)

Parker (2013) argues that the root of the problem was in the politics embedded in the design of the program, which explicitly and effectively distanced the government from the risks involved. The government, however, could not distance itself from the resultant political fallout. Once the deaths had occurred, and investigations made, it became clear that safety could not be guaranteed. The program was terminated, and public opinion on the government's role was very negative:

> The government designed the Home Insulation Program around shifting legal and financial liability from itself to the householders and installers. But what became clear in the scandal surrounding the Home Insulation Program is that in the public mind the government ultimately remained responsible for the Home Insulation Program – the safety of the houses involved and the workers who insulate them ... in the end the federal government did bear at least the reputational and moral (if not financial and legal) risks of the HIP. This can be seen in the fact that

[Prime Minister] Rudd felt compelled to take full responsibility for the failures of the Home Insulation Program in 2010, and even to issue a formal apology in 2013 to the families of the workers killed.

The government provided the funds for the program, but relied on the market to provide the services and manage the Home Insulation Program, including safety issues. Paid and unpaid domestic environmental labour was a crucial ingredient in the policy and in the market that was being stimulated by that policy. Householders who were 'purchasing' outsourced installation of insulation were assumed to be doing a great deal of technical research work, including safety risk assessments. The low-skilled labourers who were outsourced to do the paid physical work, were assumed to be employed by safety scrupulous businesses. Should householders have been expected to do the work of being 'informed buyers', not only to monitor the environmental performance of the insulation, but also the safety? Should the small businesses have expected safety regulation by government? The government was using an ecological modernization model to provide financial stimulus for the economy as a whole, but part of this model involved the transfer of risk, and implicitly, a role for domestic environmental labour in managing this risk.

The Australian federal government responsible for the program has been widely criticized. While it is known that 'green jobs' more broadly are not necessarily well paid, secure or safe (Stevis 2013), this understanding does not necessarily extend to green 'consumption' workers, otherwise known as domestic environmental labourers. Outsourcing safety risk along with environmental labour to householders and inexperienced tradespeople is unacceptable. All policy-makers concerned with domestic greening need to take into account that market mechanisms are insufficient alone to ensure safe domestic greening takes place:

> It was precisely the out-sourcing of risk to householders that led to a situation where the government was so many steps removed from the workers delivering the Home Insulation Program that it was incapable of ensuring safe work practices. This ultimately led the government to end the program prematurely and undertake a hugely expensive clean-up, compensation and work-placement program. It is interesting to note that in the controversy that engulfed the Home Insulation Program none of [the] critics suggested that more of the program could have been run by the government. The notion that a government agency could itself be capable of undertaking home insulation is completely absent from the debate. In the public debate over this failed program, the universal assumption about its delivery was that There Was No Alternative to the market.

Summary

In this chapter, I have considered some of the socio-political effects of domestic environmental labour as a largely *private* act. Since domestic greening is popular (and in policy ostensible) for *public* (environmental) good, it has been necessary to examine some of the ways the private/public interface is negotiated through labour. If the home is understood as a site that is in flux, where human–nature relations are being re-imagined, this chapter has explored some of the unfolding and shifting series of relations between householders and the broader political, economic and cultural systems to which they are materially and symbolically connected. Water tank users and off-gridders can engage in domestic environmental labour in order to increase private control over household resource use, and householders do not necessarily perceive themselves as labourers for the environment/public good. Domestic environmental labour is also implicated in power relations extending well beyond the household. Householders are discovering that their access to private land matters, for their pursuit of both green capital and individual freedom. Householders are also discovering that their voluntary household recycling-labour is indispensable in a global industry. As domestic environmental labour involves more complicated and sophisticated technologies, contractors are likely to carry out specialized labour in the home. Whoever undertakes such work, the larger political goals and green economics to which it is connected should never outweigh considerations of worker and householder protection.

References

Ahlers, R., & Zwarteveen, M. (2009). The water question in feminism: Water control and gender inequities in a neo-liberal era. *Gender, Place and Culture*, 16(4), 409–426.

Allon, F. (2008). *Renovation Nation: Our obsession with Home*. Sydney: UNSW Press.

Altmann, E. (2014). Apartments, co-ownership and sustainability: Implementation barriers for retrofitting the built environment. *Journal of Environmental Policy & Planning*, 16(4), 437–457.

Cox, R. (2013). House/work: Home as a space of work and consumption. *Geography Compass*, 7(12), 821–831.

Davison, A. (2011). A domestic twist on the eco-efficiency tum: Environmentalism, technology, home. In: A. Gorman-Murray and R. Lane (eds) *Material Geographies of Household Sustainability*. Surrey: Ashgate, 35.

Dollery, B. & Hovey, M. (2010). Australian federal government failure: The rise and fall of the Home Insulation Program. *Economic Papers: A Journal of Applied Economics and Policy*, 29(3), 342–352.

Farbotko, C., & Waitt, G. (2011). Residential air-conditioning and climate change: voices of the vulnerable. *Health Promotion Journal of Australia: Official Journal of Australian Association of Health Promotion Professionals*, 22(Special Issue), S13.

Farbotko, C., & Head, L. (2013). Gifts, sustainable consumption and giving up green anxieties at Christmas. *Geoforum*, 50, 88–96.

Farbotko, C., Walton, A., Mankad, A. and Gardner, J. (2014) Household water tanks: Mediating changing relationships with water?. *Ecology and Society*, 19(2), 62.

Gibson, C., Farbotko, C., Gill, N., Head, L., & Waitt, G. (2013). *Household Sustainability: Challenges and Dilemmas in Everyday Life*. Cheltenham, UK: Edward Elgar Publishing.

Gill, N., Osman, P., Head, L., Voyer, M., Harada, T., Waitt, G., & Gibson, C. (2015). Looking beyond installation: Why households struggle to make the most of solar hot water systems. *Energy Policy*, 87, 83–94.

Glucksmann, M. A. (2013) *Working to consume: consumers as the missing link in the division of labour*. Centre for Research in Economic Sociology and Innovation (CRESI) Working Paper 2013-03, University of Essex, Colchester, UK.

Hawkins, G. (2006). The Ethics of Waste: How We Relate to Rubbish. Lanham, MD: Rowman & Littlefield.

Kortt, M. A. & Dollery, B. (2012). The Home Insulation Program: An example of Australian government failure. *Australian Journal of Public Administration*, 71(1), 65–75.

Mee, K. J., Instone, L., Williams, M., Palmer, J., & Vaughan, N. (2014). Renting over troubled waters: An urban political ecology of rental housing. *Geographical Research*, 52(4), 365–376.

Moy, C. (2012). Rainwater tank households: water savers or water users?. *Geographical Research*, 50(2), 204–216.

Oates, C. J., & McDonald, S. (2006). Recycling and the domestic division of labour: Is green pink or blue?. *Sociology*, 40(3), 417–433.

Parker, J. K. M. (2013). *Saving Neoliberalism: Rudd Labor's Response to the 2008 Global Economic Crisis* (Doctoral dissertation). University of Technology Sydney http://hdl.handle.net/10453/29229

Pickerill, J. (2015). Cold comfort? Reconceiving the practices of bathing in British self-build eco-homes. *Annals of the Association of American Geographers*, 105(5), 1061–1077.

Shove, E. (2003). *Comfort, Cleanliness and Convenience: The Social Organization of Normality*. Oxford: Berg.

Skill, K. (2008). *(Re) Creating Ecological Action Space: Householders' Activities for Sustainable Development in Sweden*. (PhD dissertation). Linköping University: Linköping, Sweden.

Stevis, D. (2013). Green jobs? good jobs? just jobs? US labour unions confront climate change. In: *Trade Unions in the Green Economy: Working for the Environment*, London: Routledge.

Vannini, P., & Taggart, J. (2013). Voluntary simplicity, involuntary complexities, and the pull of remove: The radical ruralities of off-grid lifestyles. *Environment and Planning - A*, 45(2), 295–311.

Vannini, P., & Taggart, J. (2014). Making sense of domestic warmth: Affect, involvement, and thermoception in off-grid homes. *Body & Society*, 20(1), 61–84.

Waitt, G., Caputi, P., Gibson, C., Farbotko, C., Head, L., Gill, N., & Stanes, E. (2012). Sustainable household capability: Which households are doing the work of environmental sustainability?. *Australian Geographer*, 43(1), 51–74.

Wheeler, K. (2013) The largest environmental movement: Recycling and consumption work in Sweden, Centre for Research in Economic Sociology and Innovation (CRESI) Working Paper 2013-02, University of Essex: Colchester, UK.

Wheeler, K., & Glucksmann, M. (2015). 'It's kind of saving them a job isn't it?' The consumption work of household recycling. *The Sociological Review*, 63(3), 551–569.

4 Reclaiming domestic environmental labour

Alternative domestic green politics

Refashioning domestic green politics with creative labour: sewing and blogging

In this chapter, I tune into social media to explore an example of domestic greening in some detail: a case of ecofashion blogging, where used clothing becomes the material for a form of labour-intensive domestic upcycling. This particular example of upcycling is simultaneously a political project extending well beyond the domestic space, through online, interactive communication. In this case–study of an ecofashion blog, I wish to consider how an alternative, arguably ecofeminist, resource politics can emerge when domestic environmental labour disrupts, rather than accommodates or imitates, dominant market relations and intentionally seeks to enhance public goods in addition to private interests.

Jillian Owens describes herself as a 'writer, designer and ecofashion revolutionary'. She has an ecofashion blog with over 16,000 subscribers. The blog centres on her interest in upcycling clothing purchased cheaply from thrift stores, named Refashionista.net:

> A few years ago, I decided I wanted to change the way the world thinks about fashion. I was sickened by the rise of fast fashion giants who rely on unethical labor practices. I was worried about the impact on our planet as people tossed out their one-time-wear duds more and more quickly to make room for the newer & cheaper clothing. I was also quite broke and couldn't afford new clothes. One day, while digging through the racks at my local thrift store, I started thinking about how easily some of the ugly pieces I was looking at could be transformed into something new. I could dress well on the cheap without hurting the environment, I didn't have to support unfair labor practices, and I could have a fun new hobby!
>
> (Jillian Owens: Refashionista.net)

Upcycling clothing, for Owens, involves modifying an existing garment with techniques in the competent home-sewer's toolkit. This usually means removing and/or repurposing unwanted portions such as length, sleeves or decorations. She rarely adds additional fabric or fastenings. Owens photographs 'before' and 'after' versions of herself wearing the garment, posting these to her blog along with commentary about, and photos of, the process of modification. The reader can thus be inspired by her creative vision, as she turns ill-fitting and/or 'unfashionable' clothing, often decades old, into new versions of themselves – updated to accord more closely with contemporary fashion sensibilities. 'Before' clothing is cheekily presented in terms of both its perceived problems and its potential. For example, there may be good quality fabric, an interesting pattern or a desirable colour even if the garment (as currently configured) is unflattering, damaged or unstylish. Readers of the blog can learn from Owens' techniques for taking in, hemming, stitching, inserting elastic, and so on, as each step in the upcycle process is photographed and described with brief instructions conveyed in a light-hearted, often humorous way. Readers are able to travel with Owens on each of her refashioning journeys, from start to finish, culminating in a refashioned garments' first public appearance: Owens photographs herself wearing the finished product in social, leisure settings. Each post has the necessary elements of a good story: a challenge to the thrifted shopper's sometimes dowdy *status quo*; a struggle to make something better; suspense about whether the cuts made here and seams sewn there will culminate into something stylish and wearable; and the climax – a finished product that is transformed from another era into something that is both highly acceptable in today's fashion terms, and interesting and quirky enough to stand out from contemporary mass-produced clothing. There is always a happy ending. The new item of clothing is photographed on Owens in a fun social setting – she is admired not mocked – and all is well. Creativity and labour, the latter albeit implicit, are essential to this storyline.

For a blog's messages to be absorbed, constantly new and fresh content is needed. Owens' blog has readers returning as she transforms large quantities of thrifted clothing over time – each new post is fresh content for a growing readership. As an alternative consumption activist, her achievement is not just in having thousands read her message. It is also in having those readers acquire the inspiration and skills to reduce their own consumption of new clothes. Readers can learn new techniques to repurpose thrifted items. Owens has, somewhat remarkably, completed hundreds of refashions since commencing the blog as a side–endeavour to her full-time paid employment, in July 2010. The first few years were feverish in terms of refashioned items of clothing – one per day in the early years. Over and over again she describes in her blog entries how her many thrift shop finds are too damaged, the wrong size or simply not stylish enough for her to wear as is. While there are some 'no-sew', and relatively labour light transformations, the vast majority involve several hours of dress-making time, along with expertise, tools and physical labour to approach a version that Owens considers to be wearable. Financial benefits of refashioning are frequently mentioned by Owens: items of clothing and accessories are rarely purchased for more than US$1. We do not know much more about her domestic life from the blog. We do not know, for instance, anything about Owen's interest in other types of domestic greening. Green rhetoric is quite minimal, but a close reading of the blog posts extending over a five year period demonstrates that for Owens, refashioning second hand clothing is not a fad or a one-off, but a long-term commitment to environmentally and social responsible fashion. Her activism is largely produced in a domestic space – her sewing room – through domestic environmental labour.

Most of the blog is devoted to detailed, yet entertaining and well-edited, pictures and descriptions of processes and techniques: the cutting, pinning, unpicking, stitching and dying involved in many of her transformations. The result is a thorough documentation of her engagement in a particular type of domestic environmental labour that accords with her interpretation of an environmentally and socially responsible lifestyle. Comments on the posts are typically supportive. This work, importantly, is driven and defined by creativity and fun as well as a particular resource politics. While the labour of refashioning is crucially important to achieving her purpose, there are multiple ways in which Owens actually seeks to *deflect* attention from the considerable labour involved in each refashion. Direct comments on hard work appear only occasionally, for example:

> When I first started refashioning, there was a LOT of trial and error (mostly error).
>
> (Refashionista.net, 5 October 5 2014)

> I didn't pause to think about this [crazy uber floral frock] for very long. There was much work to do!
>
> (Refashionista.net, 4 January 2012)

More frequently, the often difficult and time-consuming work of envisioning, planning, washing, unpicking, cutting, pinning, stitching, pressing and sometimes dying the garments is downplayed, echoing in some ways the 'easy greening' narrative of ecological modernization. The focus of the blog is on the creativity and challenge in transforming old clothes into something different; the enjoyment gained from wearing the finished garment in a social setting; the private and public benefits of having a fashionable and unique wardrobe; and the financial, environmental and social benefits of a seemingly endless supply of cheap, socially and environmentally responsible clothes. Disadvantages, such as time-intensive labour, are only occasionally mentioned.

An account of 'easy greening' is made in one early blog post by focussing on the act of consumption (shopping at thrift/charity shops), rather than on the work of sewing:

> The way I look at it is, I don't have a lot of money. I can't donate as much as I would like to the charities I believe in. BUT ... I can use what spending power I have to support good causes, be green, and look fabulous...all at the same time! Just by shopping at charity shops! This idea can completely change the way we consume, and why we consume.
>
> (Refashionista.net, 26 January 2012)

This last quote supports ecological modernization's emphasis on greening through shopping. Owens' account of responsible consumption is here purportedly achieved 'just by shopping at charity shops'. Through the act of purchasing, Owens claims that it is possible for ordinary citizens to practise an ethical politics – with both environmental and social benefits. The social benefit is that buying second-hand clothes negates the need for new items made using questionable labour practices. This particular account of Owens' philosophy, however, makes no explicit mention of the significant amounts of skills, time and labour necessary to achieve her version of fashion. Yet, the practice of her politics involves significantly more than a simple purchasing decision, as evidenced in all the cutting, sewing and hemming she documents in her blog. The narrative and the activity do not quite add up. However, Owens' sewing labour does seem to separate her endeavours from the ecological modernization promise of easy greening, in practice if not in narrative. She is very clear that she has a goal to 'change the way we think about fashion' – but it does not seem to be in her interest as either a blogger or an activist to belabour the point that there is much hard work involved to achieve fashionable clothing once the charity shop purchases are brought home. Instead, she makes the labour involved more appealing using humour and consistently promoting refashioning labour as 'fun'. The blog is in many ways a parody of the fashion blogger phenomenon: Owens often makes silly faces when posing in her creations and never seems to take herself too seriously.

Interestingly, her blog portrays thrifted, refashioned clothing as desirable in a similar way to the contemporary mainstream fashion industry with other fashion bloggers – by documenting an enjoyable, real lifestyle through an online forum. Yet an important point of difference is Owens' hard work, despite her attempts to downplay this labour. Her overall collection of blog posts – hundreds in total – offers evidence that refashioning thrifted clothing is a genuine alternative to the current 'fast fashion' paradigm, where clothes are cheap, poorly made and almost 'disposable'. Owens successfully demonstrates on her blog that just about any thrift shop find can be made wearable again, but – implicitly – there is much hard work involved in making that happen, work that the consumer must do. It is the ethically acceptable and fashionable identity that Owens takes such pleasure in, however, that seems to make all the labour worthwhile.

Interestingly, Owens recreates much of the *experience* of fast fashion for herself. Fast fashion typically involves high turnover of clothing, achieving a social and psychological benefit from making new fashion statements on a regular basis. These characteristics are acceptable to Owens as long as the materials in question are not new. Their possible origin in sweatshops is not questioned – clothes seem to be cleansed of any problematic social history when acquired at a thrift store. The blog is also different to other approaches to 'sustainable fashion', some which empathize quality and longevity – akin to the slow food movement – or focus more on the sustainability of supply of new materials. Refashioning, for Owens, is different. While she takes care to ensure that nothing is wasted and every material thing finds a good home (or is stored for future use), at the same time, hers is not a slow fashion activism. She does not necessarily cherish every piece she creates, nor does she apologize for mirroring the more mainstream fast fashionista's desire for a new outfit for each occasion. Her high turnover makes for highly gripping blog reading.

In one blog post, Owens intriguingly discusses her relationship with things, claiming she has no personal attachment to the clothing she refashions. Some items are gifted by Owens to friends, others are presumably returned to thrift shops when no longer wanted. Thrifting and refashioning are an ongoing cycle for Owens, enabling her to constantly recommit to her ethical consumption but also to continually update her fashion in much the same way as mainstream fast fashionistas. She readily moves on from those items of clothing she does not enjoy looking at or wearing, even if they were the product of her labours (both shopping and sewing).

Owens sometimes simply posts online thrift store purchases – household objects for example – that require no labour to 'refashion' and interestingly, in comparison, do not make for reading that is as engaging as that documenting the creative refashions she undertakes. This is a revealing point: it is not just the finished product/item of consumption that made the earlier blog entries highly engaging – rather, it was the labour and creativity that were necessary to produce the finished product. Readers were taken on the journey of refashioning with Owens, as observers, sometimes inspired to do similar work and share them on the blog as 'reader refashions'.

From the point of view of environmental and social impact, Owens' creativity and labour are not strictly necessary to transform the consumer act of clothing oneself. Owens could achieve an equivalent or greater reduction in environmental and social impact by simply visiting a thrift store when her existing wardrobe no longer kept her warm, cool or decent due to older items wearing out. She could simply select a small number of items that fulfilled those functions, and then wear them as is until those also wore out. If Owens did not care for fashion, her sewing labours would be considerably reduced. If Owens only valued the functionality of clothing, she would not make as many thrift store purchases, there would be little creative sewing labour, and no satisfaction derived from the process of transforming something (subjectively) unfashionable into something fashionable. There would be no transfer of designing and sewing skills through the blog. There would, indeed, be a rather boring blog, with no creative ideas shared and no recognition for innovation, but environmental and social goals would still have been achieved. Owens would not have achieved the thrill and enjoyment of *fashion* on her own, more ethical terms. Fashion, and its identity politics, matter to Owens. Whether and how such cultural considerations matter more broadly in other types of domestic greening is worth exploring, particularly when additional labour is required, and particularly when the extent of that labour is downplayed in the political narrative.

Arguably, Owens' resource politics is not primarily about decoupling and retreating, as in the case of the off-gridders, or about recreating existing comforts with a reliance on new technology, which is often the resource politics of domestic water tank users – both discussed in Chapter 3. Rather, her politics is about re-energizing and repurposing existing systems of provision in a way that centralizes labour, creativity and sharing with others. Hers is an outward looking politics that makes the domestic space utterly central to transformation in resource use, and, moreover, takes domestic scale learning to the world via a blog. Owens' politics seems to be about forging better connected, creatively improved and shared resource systems, rather than barricading off privatized systems of resource use. The difference is slight, and liberal values underpin some of her work. Private interests – the fashionable self – drive much of the Refashionista endeavour, as does the private control of resources, namely, the acquisition of (used) clothing for personal benefit. But the outward facing nature of Owens' political space, achieved through public knowledge sharing, perhaps distinguishes her from the water tank owners who merely wish to beautify their garden, or the off-gridders who seem to chiefly desire disconnection from, rather than transformation and repurposing of, existing systems. It is this public politics of intentionality, an active forging of new public-private connections, that makes Owens' repurposing different to the politics of privatization that seems more commonly to shape much domestic greening. All have labour in common, and some commitment to ecological modernization. However, differences in the way domestic environmental labours are intertwined with resources, and oriented or not toward public space, seem to matter quite a lot.

Owens never assumes that technology will do most of the greening work for her. She certainly makes use of everyday domestic technology (chiefly a home computer, mobile phone to take pictures, sewing machine, scissors, unpicker, and other sewing tools). Sewing tools are often considered 'feminine'; sewing in Western traditions is work that is frequently feminized. For Owens, however, technologies of any sort play *supporting* rather than *central* roles in her resource politics. It is Owens herself who is the labourer. She puts in the vision, the creativity, the time, the energy, the knowledge, the skills, and the critical reflection. She often asks herself: did this piece successfully do what I wanted it to do? Were the attempted repurposes acceptable for style and function? Her sewing machine is never a lead character in the story. This status is reserved for herself and the garment – the resource – and the plot centres on the carefully considered, creative interactions between the self and the resource. She transforms the resource using particular tools, but those tools never substitute for the story. It is Owens and only Owens who is the labourer, and she never burdens her tools with the job of performing her green work for her.

Summary

In this chapter, I have discussed how an alternative environmental politics can emerge when domestic environmental labour materially disrupts, creatively challenges and publicly shares, rather than accommodates or imitates, dominant resource politics. The case–study of the Refashionista – refashioning used clothing as a form of labour-intensive domestic upcycling – is simultaneously a political project extending well beyond the domestic space, through the use of social media. Owens' refashioning work suggests that it is helpful to intentionally seek to enhance public goods associated with domestic labour (e.g. sewing skills) in addition to private interests when engaging in domestic greening. The question of whether Owens practises an ecofeminist politics is an interesting one. While Owens herself is not explicit about feminism on her blog, she is arguably reclaiming and repurposing traditionally feminized practices – sewing and fashion, as well as the traditionally feminized domestic space – and making them both public and political. Hers seems to be an ecofeminist politics of care, creativity, skill, labour and fun. Owens' work invites all domestic greeners to consider the creative and often enjoyable labour that is, or perhaps should be, present in other activities of domestic greening.

5 Conclusion

Nature, work, home

The labour of domestic greening: what to do when the work is too hard and technology fails

In this book, I have explored domestic environmental labour's typical absence in research and policy concerned with domestic life and its intersections with late modern environmentalism. Such an absence is significant if domestic greening, and its limitations and opportunities, are to be better understood. Throughout the book, I have discussed ways in which engagements with nature bound up in domestic consumption practices are shaped not only by technology, environmental values and politics, and household routines, but by labour as well. This, in some ways, seems like a banal point. However, while it is well-recognized that 'the home has emerged as one of the central locations for the dramatization of connections between the environment, economic change and everyday life' (Marres 2008, 30), domestic environmental labour has not been a significant part of the nexus of research into domestic greening, which is mainly understood in terms of theories of everyday practise, ecological citizenship and sustainable consumption.

Taking domestic environmental labour into account, I believe, enables increased clarity of the ways in which green goods and services deployed in domestic settings are often imagined by householders, businesses and policymakers alike, in terms of an idealized 'easy greening' through green technologies. Whether too much of the labour of reduced consumption is being ascribed to technology is a crucial issue, and this is a shared concern:

> On the one hand, eco-homes serve as instruments for articulating the involvement of subjects in environmental problems. But they are equally deployed as technologies for absolving these subjects of the ensuing responsibilities.
>
> (Marres 2008, 39–40)

In the first chapter of this book, I suggested that an idealized form of domestic environmental labour involves accessing and using water to wash and bathe *without significant depletion or pollution of the water source*; finding, nurturing, distributing, processing *and sustaining, over time*, plants and animals to eat, and materials to clothe, house, transport, entertain, and keep cool or warm members of a household or commune; keeping dirt at bay domestically and sourcing *accessible and clean* energy for cooking, heating and cooling, *without hindering others' enjoyment of cleanliness and safety*. Clearly, these ideals are difficult to achieve in daily life, but they are important aspirations nonetheless. What seems under-appreciated is that technology, particularly commercially produced technology, renders much of the labour associated with these processes less visible. Taps and pipes for water, packaged food, and other everyday technologies of modern life seem, over time, to have created a kind of technological 'third party', standing between Nature and householders. Through this relation, resources appear to be less associated with human labour and imagined more as being somehow technologically controlled; in this way resources are thoroughly politicized in a very particular way. An environmentally-focussed resource politics – usually understood as ecological modernization – appears to be technologically solvable and labour-light. Technology, it seems, is often being ascribed the responsibility for addressing the problems that arise for Nature, deemed addressable at the domestic scale.

The Enlightenment positioned homes as purportedly apolitical spaces, providing the white western male subject with the promise of a private space in which individual freedom could be enjoyed and, undesirables – both social and natural – could be excluded (Kaika 2004). It is within this ideology of the home that domestic greening in much of the industrialized North has been received: the home is imagined as a space where resources can be controlled by technology according to the notions of individual freedom of the householder. In late modernity, the home is idealized as a sanctuary of leisure. Yet this ideal does not necessarily reflect reality: homes can be sites where unpaid labour is more likely than leisure time, and where emotional and physical well-being is at risk rather than actively nurtured. There is no reason to assume that domestic greening is exempt from being part of this politics of the home, both within and external to its socially constructed boundaries.

I have spent time in this book showing the various ways in which the labour associated with domestic greening cuts across the home and into broader resource politics in multiple ways. For instance, I have considered the rather false promise that domestic labour *will* be reduced through eco-efficient technology and green consumption. I have explored that, instead, when solutions are largely consumerist and technological, information tasks are largely left to the consumer, and often end up being onerous. Yet even when such labour is experienced, there remains a tendency among producers and consumers to assume that technologies can and will do the work of conserving resources, if only their technical deficiencies can be rectified, usually through better technological information.

Within the ecological modernization project, the accumulation of capital shapes domestic environmental labour in new ways; in addition to domestic environmental labour being closely linked to broader liberal politics of the home and of resource use. Examining these processes can highlight some of the fault-lines of domestic environmental labour. The largely privatized nature of much domestic greening can sometimes lead to questionable environmental and social outcomes. Green capitalism has taken shape domestically in the shifting of part of the costs of both genuine greening of markets and greenwash to a voluntary labour force provided by householders keen to lower their environmental impact (and/or privatize access to resources) by greening their homes. It is hard work to keep the compost waste separate from the recyclables, and this separate from the landfill waste. It is hard work to maintain a solar hot water heater so that it provides both hot water when wanted *and* reduced power consumption. However, the solution is often thought to be to tinker with the machinery rather than reflect on when and why hot showers are taken. It is not, it turns out, terribly hard work to arrange installation of a backyard water tank – if you have the money and a spacious enough private property to do so. It is certainly easy to talk about saving water *and* yet also water the plants as much as before, once the tank starts storing rainwater that is unburdened by quarterly water bills.

Environmental labour studies is a newly emerging discipline, with focus to date chiefly on labour in the formal economy. Important questions remain relatively unexplored in this discipline domestically, which this book has attempted to highlight. For example, what are the practises and politics of *informal* environmental labour, particularly that which is domestic? What role does formal environmental labour carried out in domestic settings play in domestic greening? The skills required to implement some green technologies are exceptional. Highly motivated green consumers are discovering that their knowledge of complicated technologies is sometimes greater than the knowledge of the representatives of businesses who sell and advise on the installation, use and maintenance of such technologies. As green technologies for the home advance in complexity, average householders and (purportedly) green businesses may not be acquiring sufficient knowledge required to install and maintain these in the home for safety and performance. Safety and performance, it turns out, are indeed being compromised, sometimes even with lethal consequences, about which there is nothing banal or trivial: governments clearly have a strong obligation to better regulate domestic green technology industries so that health and safety standards are met.

When human health and safety is compromised, this is a clear case of ecological modernization's failure. The market for green goods is assumed to function optimally for profit and, ostensibly for the environment, a position supported by some government policies on domestic greening. However, when externalities such as worker safety and consumption work are undervalued, serious problems can emerge. Once a domestic activity becomes widely accepted as 'green', the ecological benefits of much green consumption and production associated with that activity are often taken-for-granted in the dominant version of domestic greening, at the expense of understanding who, or what, may be missing out or even harmed in the process. Negative social impacts are sometimes glossed over, not necessarily intentionally, when the *perceived* environmental benefit morally trumps the social. Not well-recognized in public debate is the shaky ground on which domestic greening activities are almost always assumed to be inherently morally worthwhile. There needs to be more questioning of the politics of domestic greening itself. 'Green jobs' – paid or unpaid, formal or informal – are not necessarily secure or safe. Understanding the unwitting, but nonetheless potentially deadly, outsourcing of domestic environmental labour to inexperienced tradespeople in a largely under-regulated industry requires new thinking: domestic environmental labour may go some way to addressing this need.

A proposition worthy of exploration, arising from the discussions in this book, may be that if domestic environmental labour is better recognized, understood and accounted for by advocates of domestic greening, then more widespread (and safe) domestic greening may take place (Cox 2013; Pink 2012). Such recognition may lead to surprising and radical unravellings of the ways in which work and environmental outcomes are intertwined. Technological innovation, for example, arguably coproduces increasing speed and busyness. When technological innovation is seen as a necessary condition for reducing environmental impacts, consistent with ecological modernization thought, by 'constant improvements towards some presumed ecological optimum way of combining natural 'resources' and human life' (Darier 1998), then speed and busyness seem to contradict constructions of the home as a space of leisure. So perhaps less reliance on technological innovation will result in additional leisure time. Further, the idea of 'slowness' might be helpful, which is neither explicit nor typical in the policy processes of sustainable consumption or in lifestyles more generally; a general reduction in human activity might reduce human-induced environmental impacts (Jalas 2012; Darier 1998). Darier (1998) points out that, along with lighter resource use as advocated in slowness movements, it might also be necessary to recognize and promote related concepts such as laziness, which currently seem antithetical to dominant capitalist values:

> The modern self is also becoming an 'environmental self', based on a general concern for 'the environment' which results in new practices related to the impact of human activity on the well-being of present and future generations of humans and other life-forms on the planet. As this environmental self is expressed within the stronger constitutive boundaries of the busy self, it does not result in a call for a general reduction in human activity. Rather it is an injunction to become busier, inventing 'cleaner' technologies, managing and planning the planet better ('sustainable development'), and evaluating present and future 'risks' (the 'Risk Society'). Consequently, contemporary modernity is often experienced simultaneously as a sense of constantly running out of time ('busy self') and that 'the planet is getting smaller and smaller' (environmental self).
>
> (Darier 1998, 194)

However, the busy self can deploy human labour in creative ways to achieve transformations, even if small scale, in resource politics. The work of upcycling can be both social and political, as well as private and material. A domestic greener can be a labourer-activist, demonstrating and publicizing the significant amounts of *human* labour required to both successfully begin to repurpose and transform an unsustainable chain of resource use at the domestic scale, and yet maintain an outward-looking, optimistic and even fun politics that seeks better connections with, rather than disconnection from, social, political and economic systems.

A focus on domestic environmental labour, then, can highlight some new ideas. It can help explain the ambivalent role of 'green technologies' in environmental citizenship. It may help householders (and policymakers) negotiate the apparent contradictions between narratives of 'easy' greening versus the realities of increased domestic labour for the environment. Greening is linked to particular commodified versions of the human-nature relationship. Currently, a strong focus of much domestic greening is on new products such as 'smart meters', water tanks, and green jeans. However, it is well-accepted in greening logic that repurposing, or other forms of extending the usefulness of objects, is important (e.g. Gregson *et al.* 2009). But not simply for material reasons (Lane and Watson 2012). Existing resources can be used in new ways, instead of extracting new ones and disposing of old ones, but the process of repurposing is fundamentally about human labour operating to implement human creativity, ingenuity, and skill. On the other hand, human–nature relations mediated by new green products and technologies are not inherently problematic; people always bring more complex cultural meanings to their interactions with such technologies than the 'leisure myth' of the corporate world might suggest. Rather, we need to be more closely attuned to the ambiguities of technologies and their nec- essary embeddedness in complex suites of social and political relations. In repurposing and upcycling, it is assumed that humans, not technology, will do the work. Typically, for new 'green' technologies, it is the other way around. Reversing this assumption would help in redirecting efforts towards socially mindful domestic greening, rather than technologically- driven 'solutions' less attuned to the possibility of negative effects such as ambivalent reductions in consumption or harms to human health.

What might be some of the effects of the 'easy greening' discourse? There is a possibility that the realities of much domestic environmental labour, particularly technological complexities, time-intensity and some- times mundane nature turn people off doing more environmental labour, because expectations of ease can subsequently turn to disillusionment with labour-intensiveness. Household recyclers can experience fatigue associ- ated with mundane tasks that do not directly return a benefit to the house- hold, and profit may be being made by others from this labour. Meanwhile, the more interesting, challenging aspects of recycling are undertaken out- side the home. For some, however, domestic greening work is voluntary work for the environment, and no matter how time-consuming, boring or complex, essentially a labour of love. The work of domestic greening is acceptable to many: a source of enjoyment and satisfaction, mentally, mor- ally and philosophically, particularly among those who are not temporally or financially stressed. However, as a social and economic service, this labour is *widely* misvalued.

Future research into domestic environmental labour should take into account social relations not deeply explored here, such as ethnicity, age and ability, as well as to more fully explore the gendered nature of domes- tic environmental labour. For many committed environmentalists, the home will likely remain a key space in which to express and practice the ver- sion of environmental citizenship that makes the most sense to them, but neglecting the labour implications of this politics may be a fundamental barrier to achieving the deep economic, political, policy and institutional change likely to be required to truly achieve a green society. Certain kinds of domestic environmental labour, particularly those which reproduce neo- liberal practices of resource privatization, can lead to a complex picture of uncertain environmental effects, sometimes worrying social outcomes, and an insular politics. Those who seem to embrace domestic environ- mental labour, focussing on the private and material aspects of resource use, through significant extra domestic work on an individual scale can nevertheless also be heavily reliant on technology to achieve much of the 'work' of privatizing resources.

Furthermore, the home idealized as a private space of leisure can stifle critical reflection, learning and communication about environmental justice. As domestic greening activities become mainstreamed, their efficacy in reducing environmental impact may simply become taken-for-granted, if technophilia trumps critical reflection on the privatization of resources and social inequities become forgotten. This is certainly not to advocate for technophobia. Rather, a healthier skepticism of much green technology as inherently 'labour-saving' and 'resource-conserving' would be helpful. Skills in the critical evaluation of science and technology, broadly, should be pursued, replacing an 'easy greening' approach. It will always be important to enable critical learning: which types of domestic environmental labour are deemed to be the most valuable and by what measures, taking into account the broader social and political effects. Perhaps most importantly, there needs to be debate about the likely limitations of complicated or commercially driven technology that promises to do the work of domestic greening. Not all green companies, green technologies or green policies are problematic, but there is much work to do in understanding their social and political entanglements, as well as their environmental effects.

Feminists in resource politics sometimes call for greater independent ownership of resources by women, although there is always the chance of dispossession (Ahlers and Zwarteveen 2009). There may be a need for greater support for women undertaking domestic greening. It is an important task for ecofeminist scholarship to document the experiences of women on whom the burden of domestic labour largely falls, and focus a critical lens on its still unfolding politics. However, this must take place with attention to the structural problems that reinforce gender inequality broadly, such as lower rates of pay, expensive childcare and non-flexible working conditions (Macgregor 2011). Perhaps, domestic environmental labour will be more likely to have positive social and environmental outcomes when not reliant on capital or sophisticated/expensive technology, when involving creativity, when there is a transformation in – rather than decoupling from – dominant systems of production and consumption, and when there is a communicative, public element extending beyond the boundaries of the domestic. Further exploration of such issues seems important in an era when aspirations to greenness often stop at installing a water tank and a solar hot water system, without much reflection on the consumption work – the domestic environmental labour – that ensues. Any 'technological fix' needs to be accompanied by cultural shift and critique, putting work into communication and creative repurposing, and reflecting on liberal ideals of leisure and privatisation of resources – perhaps for new, more public ends.

References

Ahlers, R., & Zwarteveen, M. (2009). The water question in feminism: water control and gender inequities in a neo-liberal era. Gender, *Place and Culture*, 16(4), 409–426.

Cox, R. (2013). House/work: Home as a space of work and consumption. *Geography Compass*, 7(12), 821–831.

Darier, É. (1998). Time to be lazy: Work, the environment and modern subjectivities. *Time & Society*, 7(2–3), 193–208.

Gregson, N., Metcalfe, A., & Crewe, L. (2009). Practices of object maintenance and repair: How consumers attend to consumer objects within the home. *Journal of Consumer Culture*, 9(2), 248–272.

Jalas, M. (2012). Debating the proper pace of life: Sustainable consumption policy processes at national and municipal levels. *Environmental Politics*, 21(3), 369–386.

Kaika, M. (2004). Interrogating the geographies of the familiar: Domesticating nature and constructing the autonomy of the modern home. *International Journal of Urban and Regional Research* 28(2), 265–286.

Lane, R., & Watson, M. (2012). Stewardship of things: The radical potential of product stewardship for re-framing responsibilities and relationships to products and materials. *Geoforum*, 43(6), 1254–1265.

MacGregor, S. (2011). *Beyond Mothering Earth: Ecological Citizenship and the Politics of Care*. Vancouver: UBC Press.

Marres, N. (2008). The making of climate publics: Eco-homes as material devices of publicity. *Distinktion: Scandinavian Journal of Social Theory*, 9(1), 27–45.

Pink, S. (2012). *Situating Everyday Life: Practices and Places*. Los Angeles: Sage.

Index

Taylor & Francis eBooks

Helping you to choose the right eBooks for your Library

Add Routledge titles to your library's digital collection today. Taylor and Francis ebooks contains over 50,000 titles in the Humanities, Social Sciences, Behavioural Sciences, Built Environment and Law.

Choose from a range of subject packages or create your own!

Benefits for you

>> Free MARC records
>> COUNTER-compliant usage statistics
>> Flexible purchase and pricing options
>> All titles DRM-free.

REQUEST YOUR FREE INSTITUTIONAL TRIAL TODAY

Free Trials Available
We offer free trials to qualifying academic, corporate and government customers.

Benefits for your user

>> Off-site, anytime access via Athens or referring URL
>> Print or copy pages or chapters
>> Full content search
>> Bookmark, highlight and annotate text
>> Access to thousands of pages of quality research at the click of a button.

eCollections – Choose from over 30 subject eCollections, including:

Archaeology	Language Learning
Architecture	Law
Asian Studies	Literature
Business & Management	Media & Communication
Classical Studies	Middle East Studies
Construction	Music
Creative & Media Arts	Philosophy
Criminology & Criminal Justice	Planning
Economics	Politics
Education	Psychology & Mental Health
Energy	Religion
Engineering	Security
English Language & Linguistics	Social Work
Environment & Sustainability	Sociology
Geography	Sport
Health Studies	Theatre & Performance
History	Tourism, Hospitality & Events

For more information, pricing enquiries or to order a free trial, please contact your local sales team:
www.tandfebooks.com/page/sales

Routledge
Taylor & Francis Group

The home of
Routledge books

www.tandfebooks.com